Peng

Get

Kaz Cooke is an Australian cartoonist, author and newspaper columnist. Her publications include *Real Gorgeous: the Truth about Body and Beauty*; *Keep Yourself Nice*; *The Modern Girl's Guide to Safe Sex*; *The Modern Girl's Diary* series; *The Crocodile Club* and, most recently, the *Great Hysterical Figures Calendar*. Her cartoon character, Hermoine the Modern Girl, features in many of Kaz's books, in the short animated film *Gorgeous* and the CD-ROM *Totally Gorgeous*.

To Dear Deirdre
Lots of Love
From Glenys
Christmas 1996

For Geoffrey

Get a Grip

Kaz Cooke

PENGUIN BOOKS

Penguin Books Australia Ltd
487 Maroondah Highway, PO Box 257
Ringwood, Victoria 3134, Australia
Penguin Books Ltd
Harmondsworth, Middlesex, England
Viking Penguin, A Division of Penguin Books USA Inc.
375 Hudson Street, New York, New York 10014, USA
Penguin Books Canada Limited
10 Alcorn Avenue, Toronto, Ontario, Canada M4V 3B2
Penguin Books (N.Z.) Ltd
182–190 Wairau Road, Auckland 10, New Zealand

First published by Penguin Books Australia Ltd 1996
1 3 5 7 9 10 8 6 4 2
Copyright © Kaz Cooke, 1996

All rights reserved. Without limiting the rights under copyright reserved above, no part of this publication may be reproduced, stored in or introduced into a retrieval system, or transmitted, in any form or by any means (electronic, mechanical, photocopying, recording or otherwise), without the prior written permission of both the copyright owner and the above publisher of this book.

Typeset in 11.7/16pt Weiss by Post Typesetters
Original front cover black and white photograph: Athol Shmith
Back cover photograph: AAP Photo Library
Printed and bound in Australia by Australian Print Group, Maryborough
Printed on Australian-made Regent 100% Recycled Offset paper

National Library of Australia
Cataloguing-in-Publication data
Cooke, Kaz, 1962– .
Get a grip.
ISBN 0 14 026343 8.
Title.
032

Contents

Acknowledgements ix

1 Completely Frocked Up 1
Shock Horror Size 14 3
The Ironing of It All 6
Wedding Bells for Ding-dongs 9
Corset and Effect 12
Get a Grip 15
Into the Valley of Over Thirty Rode the Hairy Ones 18
Bad Taste Is In 21

2 Sex and Possibly Romance 25
The Man Wees at the Lady 27
Spring Is Sprunged 30
Happy as a Clam 33
Snoring 36
Great Expectations 39
Mothers-in-Law 42

3 Ads and Other Fat Fibs 45
You Beauty Industry Seminar 47
The Hydration of Firmly-Sue 50
The Adulation of the Anorexi 53
Men: Hold on to Your Willy 56
What New Woman? 59

Get a Loada the Cars on Miss Venezuela 62
A Cracked Force 65
A Short History of Excuses, Excuses 68

4 Politicking 71
Shut Up about Political Correctness 73
Shut Right Up 76
Bazza You Legend 79
Is That a Bermb in Your Pocket, Cheri? 82
Feral Policymakers on the Loose 85
Taxing Time 88
The Real Australian History 92

5 Spirituality and Other Dippiness 95
My Tiny Shoulder Is Frozen 97
Hippy Drippy 100
Hello? 103
Finding Your Inner Nanna 106
Fantasy Section 109
Ho, Ho, Ho Mary Christmas 112
Pope-ular Misconception 115

6 The Creativish Arts 119
Fair Enough Cobber Blue Beaut Mate 121
To Whom It May Concern 124
Lost in the Translation 127
Is That a Chicken in Your Pocket or
Are You a Conceptual Artist? 130
Jane Where Are Your Nipples: Video Reviews 133
A Shameful Addiction to Wicker 136
What's My Line? 139

7 Oeuvre-indulgence 143
Nuevo Foodo 145
White Christmas Dreaming 151

Ho, Ho, Berloody Ho   154
Passive Parenting   157
'Tis the Season to Drink Bolly   160
Grunge Gambling   163
The Peerless Fearless   166

8 Women's Rites   169
Berloody Feminists   171
Uneasy Lies the Head That Wears the Big Tiara Thingie   174
Pretty Implausible Woman   177
Provoking Insights   180
Up Yours Cazaly   183
Dealing with Heels   186

9 Travels with My Id   189
A Real Trip   191
Don't Put Your Daughter on the Plane   194
Jet Lag   202
Hayseed Holiday Hints   205
C'mon Baby, Do the Aviation   208
Helena Handbasket   211

10 Blathering On   215
Warning: Warnings   217
A Slew of Collective Nouns   220
Hello, Hello, Hello   224
Cats Suck   227
Gratuitous Koala Bashing   230
Just Testing   233
To Boldly Go on the Blink   236
School Reports   239
Names and Addresses   242

Acknowledgements

Most of the items in this book were first published as columns in the *Sydney Morning Herald* and the *Sunday Age*. I would like to thank in particular the inaugural section editors, respectively Lauren Martin and Garry Linnell, and all the editors since, especially ones called Ken Merrigan and Amanda Wilson. I would also like to thank Michael Shmith for permission to use his father Athol's photographic portrait of Princess Panda, a television star of the 1950s and 1960s. The photograph appears on the front cover.

1
Completely Frocked Up

Shock Horror Size 14

I tried to buy a size 14 pair of trousers last week. Oh, call me crazy. I know, it was a mad, impetuous whim; I was asking for trouble, I don't know WHAT came over me: just not concentrating, I suppose. In the first shop, the woman looked puzzled. She was surrounded by itty bitty hankies made from PVC and other extruded plastics, called 'clothes'.

There *was* a size 14 garment in the shop, she discovered. It was a red plastic miniskirt that would just about cover somebody's map of Tasmania, but not if you were ever in the habit of, say, sitting down. There was a pair of trousers claiming to be a 14 in another shop. The thigh region had just enough fabric to wrap up a toothbrush, and one's buttocks would have to be housed interstate for the duration.

You can imagine the thrill I felt in the thirty-eighth shop when I saw some trousers cut for a woman's shape (in, out, then in again: a difficult concept in the fashion industry). My trembling fingers prised open the waistband. Twelve. Sometimes one can get into a 12 when one is a 14, but generally speaking this is a folly designed to make grown women break down and sob in the change rooms, which are usually flooded by the kind of lighting hardware necessary for micro-surgical procedures performed in a warehouse.

'Have you got these in a size 14?' I asked. Sure, it was a masochistic urge. But I wanted a pair of trousers. And I'm not in the least upset at being a size 14. It's just that it seems to upset shop assistants. They get giddy at the thought of a number that big, and have to lie down, nibbling occasionally on some curly endive leaves for a few days. Still, I risked it. Luckily, this assistant was made of stern stuff. 'FOURTEEN?' she replied quizzically, as a disbelieving hush fell over the shop and young women hid among racks stretching to the horizon of size 8 straight-leg polyester pants and crop tops that might fit a Barbie doll if she had a breast reduction. 'We had some 14s in the first week, but they go really quickly.' Der.

I finally fell, weeping, into a designer shop, and found two pairs of size 14 pants with enough room for legs. They were approximately $127,000 each. The assistant here agreed that the situation was dire. 'I keep arguing with my friend, who buys clothes for women's wear chain stores. He says this year everything is really tight and tiny with unnatural colours and fabrics but next year things will be big and floppy again.'

Well, natch. Because by this time next year women will have thrush all over their entire bodies from wearing bits of tight plastic, and will be forced by their doctors to buy large cotton things the size of cinema curtains. This season's clothes are not so much baby doll as a baby's doll's. I do not wish to wear a crop top and a skirt the size of a business card. I'm funny like that.

HELLO? Message to the fashion industry. I'll speak slowly, and carefully. If your three size 14s sell in the first week, and you then spend weeks and weeks with immoveable containerloads of size 10s and enough size 8s to fill the Katherine Gorge, why don't you make some comfortable trousers that look good on a size 14 woman? WE... WILL... GIVE... YOU... MONEY.

I realise that it may be painful for you to understand that some people with hips bigger than Linda Evangebloodylista's head might want to wear some clothes, but try to keep up. Supply and demand only works if somebody keeps their end up in the supply department and provides something we can get our end into.

The Ironing of It All

Somewhere at our place there's an iron. It might be in the cupboard with all the plastic thingies with missing lids, or it might be in the cupboard with mozzie candles, parade inspection boot polish for those heavy days, and plastic lids with missing thingies. There is a possibility of it being at the bottom of the bathroom cupboard behind the emergency supplies of lint.

My Nanna would be horrified at this, were she with us still. She used to iron hankies, ribbons, woollen scarves, pillow cases, sheets, jeans and curtains. She ironed underpants, and singlets, and passing traffic. She would iron your hair if you were curly, and curl it if it was straight. Once I saw her ironing a travel rug. She was quite unhinged about ironing, by today's standards.

It has taken me several years, but I have eventually eliminated ironing from my life. Only rarely do I look wistfully at somebody else's ironed hanky, much as I used to gaze at other kids' playlunches at primary school. They had cakie things, and mysterious sticky buns with severe icing involvement. (Little tarts that were pink on one side and chocolate on the other!) My playlunch had dried apricots and wholegrain grape sandwiches. (If any further evidence should be required of recurrent madness in my family, the grapes were cut in half so they wouldn't roll around in the sandwich.)

Once, in Grade 3, I accidentally stole Tom Coleman's lunch and was halfway through the jam tart thinking that Mum had lost her mind, but in a really good way, when Tom Coleman found me, thumped me, and threw me my real paper bag full of figs and a grated carrot surprise. (Later on, in Grade 6, I knocked bits of Tom Coleman's front teeth right into tonsil-land with a drumstick during a percussion tragedy. It was then I started to believe in fate, and abandoned my career as an elegant drummer.)

If I were confined to a dungeon (or, as we now call them, work-station area) and I could only escape by spinning my hair into gold under an enterprise bargaining agreement, or perfectly ironing a button-down, rufflefront, pleated business shirt with double cufflink function, I could make good my escape in the twinkling of a steam iron on the linen setting. My mother trained me well. It's just that I'd rather not.

My latest paramour, the dashing Mr Des Tiny, is far more shackled to the smoothing iron. He is trapped by the weird social rules that demand that he dress befitting a man in his trade (head wiglet-wrangler at Mistress Beverley Bouffant's Discreet Hairpieces: A Bit of Shoosh about Your Joosh, all major credit cards not only accepted but fallen upon with cries of inarticulate joy). Winter and summer, men are expected to front in a well-appointed smirking jacket, with a matching, cuffed trouser, a shirt of business, and a necktie of an amusing and intimidating hue.

Come each pearly-faced dawn, Des Tiny stands on his mezzanine decking clad only in pyjamery and slippery, the personification of slightly cerulean splendour, ironing into a stiff, icy breeze, hooked up to the generator, steaming up his helmet and putting the art back into the dart. He's a padded hangover from the days when accredited wiglet wranglers had valets to iron their own shirts.

We must save Des and his ilk from this appliance slavery. If your clothes make a statement, say it loud and say it proud: 'I'm sort of quite rumpled!' We will shortly be moving to phase two of our campaign: elasticised waists, the use of the beret in postponing hairwashing and getting the most out of stretch pants.

Wedding Bells for Ding-dongs

This morning I fell across a copy of a magazine called *Collections Including Veils and Headpieces* (186 pages: the paper cuts were horrendous). Blanche, honey, there's much to be purchased, if you're still planning to get merged with Mr Hawke on Sunday. (Alert book readers will recall the splicing of former prime minister Robert Hawke and his biographer, Blanche d'Alpuget.)

As you know, I am a very enthusiastic supporter of the idea that the wedding day is the most important one in a woman's life. For example, you get to wear a tiara without the relatives saying, 'Stop putting on the dog and take a long, hard look at yourself my girl'. The only important thing is the day itself. No, I lie. The important thing is what you wear on the day itself, and how much it costs.

You'll be thankfully over the preliminaries by now. (My most enduring memory of an engagement party is the stoic look on the face of a bride to be in West Altona carrying a bucket of her betrothed's vomit to the toilet. A teetotaller, his drinks had been spiked by his best mates. As far as I could tell, the publishers of *Bride to Be* – and

Collections Including Veils and Headpieces — have yet to address this problem. It could detract from the glamour.)

Anyway, at $11.95 *Collections* is a steal for seeing 56,7893,637 bridal gowns, some of which will get you change of $4000. I particularly enjoyed Alan Pinkus's analysis of wedding shoes: 'Toe shapes are pointed, oblique, round and bumped, all featuring spiky to solid heels with straight and curved silhouettes'. (Alan does not say so explicitly but one imagines that they are worn on the feet.) I thought Alan was a shoe journalist but it turns out Alan Pinkus runs a shoe shop! Life is so full of coincidences!

As you know, Blanchey, I am a sucker for a grouse tiara, and there are many to choose from. There is a halo style (warning, warning); 'Camelot'; the 'Fairy Tale' (run for your life); 'a cloud of crystals and pearls' not to mention the finish in gold-edged fluted tulle at the back. (You could probably save some money if you fluted the tulle yourself. Of course you'd have to know a bit about tulle-fluting.)

As well as the traditional gorgeous wedding gowns, with acres of tulle (some of it, sadly, quite unfluted) and trains approximately the length of the Orient Express route, there are some gowns for the wilder at heart. Some of them are pink! One of them is black satin with a feather boa wrapped around the bonce! (What are you trying to do, KILL the aunties?!) The French lace on page 90 'explodes into 35 metres of silk organza'. (Typical.)

But if I know you, Blanche, you'll stick to something simple, very, very private and traditional, perhaps in white towelling, although you might consider a bustle. You can't go past a girl with big false botty, as far as I'm concerned. If you're going to be playing the part of a princess for a day, you'll be wanting some serious buttock enhancement.

It's lucky you're getting in before the republic. This is your last chance for a royal touch: Queen Anne neckline, Elizabeth tiara, duchess satin, Empire line bodice, Princess A-line frock, regal tiara, princess satin, and screaming Prince Edward flouncy-pants. Oh, all right, I made that last one up. Whatever you do, make sure you're kitted out properly. You can forget your lines if you like, but the solemn bond between you and the photographers is not to be trifled with.

But don't take my word for it. Ask the people who are trying to sell you this stuff. And do remember, it's the happiest day of your life. (I'm sorry to break the news, but word is it'll be all downhill after that.)

Corset and Effect

Apparently the corset is back. (Nobody is exactly sure where the corset went, possibly on a caravan holiday to Bega.) Fashion writers, fresh from dowdy hors d'oeuvre at the launch of 'grunge' clothes, are trumpeting (not like a trumpet trumpets, like an elephant trumpets) the return of 'glamour'.

It seems that all these things now 'back' have been locked up in a home for wayward fashion fancies until their parole came up. Platform shoes were given early release some time ago, but have constantly offended since. Sex is back (hello?), culottes are in solitary confinement and the poodle perm got life.

Now glamour is out on the lam, with unkissable glossy lips and acrobatic curls and padded bras, and clothes that are scrinchy-tight and shoes that make you want to cry a lot. This, of course, will be superseded shortly by something called 'The New Reality' or 'The Natural Look' or 'Maybe Now We Can Convince Them They Need Beige Tracksuit Pants Instead, What Do You Think, Raoul?' In the meantime, glamour is being marketed as Femininity.

Femininity, a characteristic which all women are supposed to aspire to, is rather a slippery term. Does It mean Girly? Does It mean Womanly? Is It something all women have by birthright? Or do you have to spend $4000 on some frilly see-through flouncy-drawered resort-wear to attain It?

According to the fashion pundits (from the Latin, *mug punter*), femininity seems to have something to do with it hurting. Now that glamour and corsets are back we can embrace our femininity once more, while pretending it isn't killing us. (Because Lord knows, girls, aren't you sick to death of just being comfortable with a haircut that suits you and wearing the make-up you like and just frocking up for a party?)

Smirk seductively as you strap yourself into a tighter-than-wetsuit rubber Lycra corset: squish those ovaries and give a great big jaunty welcome to irritable bowel syndrome and bruised ribs. Laugh in a tinkly, breathy, sort of a non-threatening way as you crush your feet into some stilettos and give free rein to alluring bunions, ankle injuries and thrown vertebrae!

We're not just talking boring old lippy, we're whispering sweet, pliant nothings as we hold the lippy in place with a chemical sibling of clear nail polish, yum! Purr languidly as you hoist your boosies to about clavicle level while the Wonder Bra straps leave lovely angry welts in your shoulders! Sexily slink to the boudoir and sleep in hair-rollers (well, lie down in them, anyway) and oooh

Completely Frocked Up

I do beg your pardon, I seem to be having an LSD flashback.

Australian clothes designer Trent Nathan is quoted as saying, 'And so wonderful to see women's bosoms again' (Trent, there are magazines you can buy for that), and somebody called Sheila Scotter said of rubber corsetry in her past, 'Of course it was agony and artificial, but fashion is an artifice and sometimes you have to suffer. I think it is about time we paid more attention to being feminine'. And I believe that's a giant sardine at my front door trying to sell me a copy of *The Watchtower*.

The bad news is if you're not into this kind of Do-It-Yourself S & M right now, you're unfashionable. The good news is by tomorrow they'll be trying to flog us something else. And the best news of all is that it's the True Fashion Believers who are going to hurt themselves in corsets: and that's the perfect revenge on the designers and fashion writers. No, go right ahead, gang, corset yourselves stupid. We'll all be having a daiquiri over here, laughing our heads off. And we'll be feeling no pain.

Get a Grip

The Comedy Festival is one thing, but fashion pages can have you going the giggle year round, and all for the cost of a newspaper, or the risk of getting bounced at the newsagency for overzealous browsing. Last week I managed to get off the floor quite soon after reading an hilarious article about handbags.

Most women I know spend some portion of their lives (usually their twenties) looking for the perfect handbag. It's got to be able to fit everything you might want during the course of a day (except a good lie down, a long, hard look at yourself, a damned good kissing and a chocolate ice cream) without being a steamer trunk. On the other hand, it should be big enough to find during a panic and not be confused with one of Barbie's accessories, like Ken.

One friend did used to carry around a small suitcase, which became unwieldy, so now she just stays at home most of the time. Some people carry briefcases or backpacks, but it depends on the job. My brother doesn't need a briefcase because he uses a Kombi van. I can remember, too, experiments with teeny, tiny handbags with room enough for an American Express Gold Card and a wafer, which would have been completely peachy if any of us had a credit card or a wafer.

Then there was a short burst of see-through plastic or mesh briefcases. This proved too much of a strain because you could only carry around witty and smart objects, like *Wonder Woman* comics or the kind of stuff you find in design shops that are stark and Italian and streamlined and completely bloody useless, like a $475 eye de-glazer with triple tong function.

Also, see-through briefcases are no good for carrying around the more embarrassing bits a Modern Girl needs in her kit. In my case this includes twenty-seven lipsticks, all the envelopes I never open because they have little windows on them and as such are always bad news, a stout etiquette volume, occie straps, a spare pair of boots, tissues, Band-Aids, keys, small icons from the Mesopotamian era, reams of unfathomable notes saying 'light bulbs, milk, sump oil', quite a bit of orange peel and some herbal tablets for stress induced by trying to find something in my handbag.

Anyway, in this fashion article it said that an author called Joanne Finkelstein reckons that carrying a handbag 'suggests a lack of self-enclosure, a lack of self-sufficiency, as if the human body cannot support itself'. I suspect Joanne has had too much university in one go, and she's probably the type to have a clean hanky pinned to her bra strap and a quantity of cash glued to the inside of her rain bonnet. Perhaps it is also a key to her Joanne-ness that her essay on this subject is titled 'Codpieces'.

Even more distressing was the revelation that one's handbag says something sexual about one, although no actual analysis was made of the significance of orange peel and boots. There used to be an ad (a precursor to the I'm-pretty-famous-and-this-is-what-I-keep-on-my-Powerbook campaign) that said, 'You can tell a lot about (celebrity girly person) by what's in her Glo-mesh bag'. You couldn't though, because it was all art-directed and obviously none of them ever had periods or had to buy sump oil and they always had photos of men with big jaws who looked like they might be called Garth from marketing.

Frankly, I think we can have too much of this kind of psychology. At a wild guess, I'd say most people carry a handbag they like so they can put stuff in it. If you can't get a handle on it, get a grip. I've got that written down somewhere.

Into the Valley of Over Thirty Rode the Hairy Ones

By way of warning, some awful stuff happens to you on the other side of thirty.

Truly Horrible Truth One
You can no longer dance until five o'clock in the morning, take vast quantities of alcohol and at least two other restricted substances if you count tobacco, and I find these days one does, and then spring out of bed like a gilded lily ready for work. In fact, once you're over thirty, two glasses of alcoholic beverage is just this side of blathering-idiot land. Three glasses, university tests prove, in a woman over thirty causes her to whiffle on indelicately until she empties the room or crashes insensible into the shrubbery, utterly giltless.

Truly Horrible Truth Two
You turn into a raving pervert in ill-fitting slingbacks. This is because your feet get bigger as you get older and also because of the fact that you just honestly turn into a slathering sleaze of a woman for no apparent reason apart from the aforementioned overthirtyness.

For example, you may have spent some conversations in your life deploring the way that women are consistently portrayed as sex objects in advertising and other media. Once you are over thirty this will not stop you moaning 'Oh God, yes, yes, *yes!*' when you watch the Richmond players run onto the MCG in some rather new-fashioned nylon shorts that inevitably give rise to grave concerns about chafing.

In fact, you may find, if you are a straight Modern Girl over thirty, that your interest soars in any team sports involving partly clothed Adoni and of course the noble tradition of the game. You will also begin noticing that police constables are uniformly twelve years old but that male fire officers hold a fascination that is not so much about arson but sheer light-headed girly worship.

I'm not saying this is right. I'm just warning you, in case you're not yet thirty. I don't want you to be any more rudely shocked than you have to be. You will by then have worked out that it's best to sleep with someone you can have a conversation with, but this will not stop you salivating in public in a most unseemly way. (It is no good pretending that your appreciation is merely artistic. They can see right through us.)

Truly Horrible Truth Three
On the other side of thirty there is a moustache waiting. And maybe a wee little beard, and possibly other tufty bits of a slightly disconcerting nature. Luckily it is probably hardly noticeable unless you go into one of those public

toilets with 356,000 watt Kleig fluoro lighting that make you look like Godzilla and then incidentally when you go into the cubicle the toilet roll dispenser is completely encased in a metal rectangle and you have to poke up through a little slot with your fingertip and awkwardly twist around the toilet roll until you can grab an end and then you pull it gently, gently through the slot and after 2 centimetres it breaks: snap! Why would anyone design a thing like that? Anyway, one of the things that happens over thirty is that your concentration begins to wander.

Truly Horrible Truth Four
Because of substance abuse and anaesthetic use during your twenties you will find there are three brain cells left: Francine, Ern and Brenda. Francine does the right side of the brain, Ernie the left, and Brenda knows where the keys are. We mourn the tragic passing of Ian, who used to fit names to faces. (Ian, of course, was lost during the hideous Tia Maria/Mullumbimby Heads incident of 1987.)

Frankly, that's the great thing about being in your thirties – you've really found who you are: a mohair-faced slavering gasbag two-pot screamer flat-footed bore. What a relief.

Bad Taste Is In

Readers of the February edition of US *Harpers Bazaar* magazine (yes, I know it's May now, but it's only just hit the hairdresser's, okay?) will gain a remarkable insight into the psyche and intelligence of a fashion designer, if one is permitted to use all those words in the same sentence, especially 'intelligence' in such close proximity to 'fashion designer'.

Frock designer Jean Colonna was quoted about a very hideous outfit he had made. 'These fabrics are all the ones that have a bad reputation: leatherette, nylon, scratchy jersey, prints that are disturbing. Street people are an unlimited source of inspiration to me, the way they mix everything.' (The jacket is $450, the skirt is $205, the 'camisole' $375. For Australian prices, add about a third.)

In the ever-decreasing circle of fashion, the 'style makers' can ping-pong between 'glam-trash' and 'geek-chic' and tear a skirt length up and down like a roller blind, all in the space of your average afternoon tea. They are desperate for something new. 'When Chanel becomes what people think Chanel should be, then we need polyester', says Karl Lagerfeld in the same magazine. Chanel has, of

Completely Frocked Up

course, become exactly what people think it is, which is hellishly expensive. (Will making ugly clothes out of uncomfortable, unflattering fabrics lower the prices? What do you reckon?)

The fabulously named designer Anna Demeulemeester is so out of ideas she admires what she hates: 'Sometimes the thing you dislike the most can be the most inspiring – it forces you to get a grip'. (By 'grip' she probably means a new handbag.) When all else has been plundered for catwalk ideas, why not look, like Jean Colonna, to the poorest of the poor for inspiration? Is this not a triumph: working out a way to steal from those who have the least? The resulting homeless look is called 'Bad Taste Fashion' – in other words, bad taste is 'in'.

If the designers call the *clothes* 'bad taste', heaven knows how they categorise their own attitudes. How far can bad taste in ideas go? Can we confidently predict the new homeless style on the catwalk: models urinating on stage, feigning the seemingly random shouting of a psychotic episode and generally getting right into the new-found chic of being entirely without respect, power or Louis Vuitton luggage?

Models have a great head start: many of them are already achingly thin, with big, sticky-out elbows and knees, and they're used to being made up to look like strung-out junkies who have spent the night in a skip. They have been magically enhanced by a bit of cadaver-white make-up on their face, and a refreshingly light blue lipstick (perhaps they could call it 'Emergency Room

22 Get a Grip

Blue'), and artfully applied grey around and under the eyes, and their hair sprayed down into matted clumps of unkempt perfection. Are we going to witness the supermodels, fake fingernails flying, mugging homeless people to get the clothes off their backs at their next gigs?

Of course not – no need to get that close. What are photographers for, darlings? Besides which, the homeless as fashion fad will probably last until next Thursday. Well, truthfully, it probably went out and came back in and went out again while this column was being typeset.

The next time a homeless person asks you to part with some loose change, maybe you could go that one extra step. 'Say, where did you get that FABulous beanie! And that great old jumper with the wittily arranged soup stains! I saw one just like it in Italian *Marie Claire*! Oh My God! aren't you . . . Cindy Crawford?' And remember – don't forget to give to the Salvos and the other homeless charities: you'll get a toasty glow just knowing that you've helped a famous fashion designer have a thought.

2
Sex and Possibly Romance

The Man Wees at the Lady

Condom machines in schools are not the only answer to sexually transmitted diseases and unwanted pregnancy, any more than you can stop after eating just one Tim Tam. How to say 'No' to sex needs to be taught in schools too. (Then again, I was taught long division at school. Couldn't do it now to save my life.)

If only every school had classes that emphasise self-esteem, the confidence that only comes with knowledge, and the right to wait until you're ready: the emotional and the scientific sides of sex. Many people – not just teenagers – confuse attention with approval, Tim Tams with breakfast, sex with love, a boyfriend or girlfriend with security or growing up.

But many schools, especially 'religious' ones, have no relationships or sex education at all. Thousands of parents never discuss it except perhaps for a fumbled, 'You know about, er, how to change a tyre, and, er, sex, don't you?'. 'Yes, Dad, shut up.' Blushes all round. I can remember a girl at school explaining firmly how 'the man wees at the lady and the baby bursts out of the tummy button a bit later'. She must have been very relieved, or perhaps just very pregnant, when the truth finally sank in. (And I bet she couldn't sit through *Alien*.)

So many kids think you can't get pregnant the first time, or if you're standing up. Or they believe that their natural sexual urges are disgusting and worthy of self-loathing and guilt. They get drunk or stoned for the first time and get into dangerous situations. They believe that you don't need a condom if you really love the other person, or you trust your partner, or you're in a long-term relationship. (As I cast my mind back to Year 10, a long-term relationship was anything longer than lunchtime. Actually, if I cast my mind back a year or two, I remember that a long-term relationship lasted about as long as baby carrots left out of the crisper.)

According to a recent Victorian survey, almost 40 per cent of school kids are having sex by Year 11. More than a third of 79,000 of abortions in 1990 were performed on teenaged girls, poor darlings. God knows how many more kids contracted chlamydia, gonorrhea, the wart virus (which can lead to cervical cancer) and probably didn't even know it. Herpes is on the rise again.

Is this 'appropriate' punishment for kids who want to say 'Yes', or who wanted to say 'No' but were frightened, or confused, or intimidated? If the moral minority truly believe this, they should just come right out and say so. They should call for young people who are caught having sex to be injected with the HIV virus as 'godly' revenge. If condoms are 'inappropriate' for teenagers, they should say that it is 'appropriate' for a thirteen-year-old girl to give birth to a child and educate it for life. They should say it is just that a young boy should have to deal with the fact that his girlfriend had to 'choose' an abortion, even though he wasn't sure why. Because these are the inarguable results of ignorance and no contraception.

Kids are embarrassed to face a doctor or buy condoms at supermarkets and chemists — public places, maybe in a small town, or maybe where their parents shop. It could even be embarrassing buying condoms from the school toilets — schools being hotbeds more of gossip than anything else. But it's a start. Condoms need to be everywhere: in schools, shopping mall toilets, home bathrooms, anywhere somebody might grab a moment of privacy and a handful of protection. Condom machines need to become no big deal, unremarkable and ubiquitous.

Because, lordy, lordy, teenagers are going to have sex. And, hallelujah, nobody should have to die of embarrassment.

Spring Is Sprunged

Ahh, Spring, when the daffodils riot (just *where* are the daffodil riot police when you need them?) and the younger womenfolk start showing their pierced navels. Any swelling and subsequent gangrene, presumably, has cleared up during the year's more arctic portion.

A sprung Spring would also account for the appearance on the magazine shelves of *Flirt!*. *Flirt!* magazine (love the exclamation mark) carries an ad that rates romantic fiction novels from four lipstick imprints (romantic) to six (fiery). An example of six lippy imprints is Cecile Kingsley who is taught by Dr Rand Coursey to love again. (Presumably she also learned to laugh again if she had to call him Dr Randy.)

Despite the mortification of actually taking notes from *Flirt!* on public transport, I waded through the ads, from the tantalising prospect of working for Tiffany's escort service ('the freedom of being self-employed . . .') to Avon's 'eye perfector' cream. Tragically, this is not an ointment to make you more of a discerning perv. 'Baggy, puffy eyes can be a rude awakening first thing in the morning', apparently.

In other words, don't send that stranger screaming the next morning because you look like Donald Pleasance in the peepers department. Spread some fat on them instead, or as Avon calls it, liposomes. (Thrifty hint: use bacon fat instead and you won't have to buy him breakfast.)

I lack all of the flirting clobber in the fashion pages: a hot-pink fake-fur jacket made of the sort of material used for those fluffy toilet-seat covers; purple fishnet stockings; a feather-boa-trimmed jacket and a nice grey cardy. What would be the use of meeting with somebody in the dating service columns? The 'Elle Macpherson lookalike' who has 'fishing fantasies' might hate my cardy. Better to stick with the phone services in case I want to ring somebody who pretends I am licking her stilettos. (Euwww.)

A *Flirt!* article says 'studies have demonstrated time and time again that women become attracted to men who listen to them, look at them and seem to be genuinely interested in them'. (Other studies demonstrate that some women are attracted to the man with the least teeth and the most tattoos, or the ones who have a wife, three girlfriends and a bulk discount at the local childcare centre. Others might sleep with anybody who asks nicely in a Scottish accent. Which is why I must never go to Scotland. Imagine the scene in Customs: 'Madam, have you anything to declare?' 'Yes! I must have you!'.)

Elsewhere it says the transformation caused by kissing makes one feel that 'deep down, you know you are . . . the statuesque slut on the beach, her buttocks bisected by a

G-string'. I am going to have to speak to my Fancy Man, Des Tiny, about this. When I kiss him I am more often convinced I am wearing a tracksuit and some carpet slippers in a car park. The idea of being a statuesque slut with third-degree sunburn on my botty hardly comes into it, sadly. If I really concentrate, perhaps I can imagine I am a short, solid floozy in a pair of sensible Speedos near a wading pool.

It was even more disquieting in the horoscopes section to find that as a Sagittarian I am constantly in a state of semi-arousal and I am half woman, half creature of the glen (Glen who?), and a likely candidate for group sex. I'll have you know that shame and jealousy have no lasting effect on me. Des, on the other hand, is pegged as a Gemini man, who 'has a compulsion to satisfy a woman every time'. But the 'tedious lengths' he goes to usually 'dampen the spark'. Well, he can show me his tedious lengths any time, darling.

Golly, it must be Spring.

Happy as a Clam

When this column was asked how it was feeling recently, it replied, 'Happy as a clam', an old American expression of dim origins. Challenged on the question of exactly how blissful a bi-valve could be, it became imperative to investigate.

For the purposes of getting through the exercise in less than eight years, it is the giant clam we take as our subject today.

Professor John Lucas of the Zoology Department of James Cook University in Townsville, who sounds gorgeous, was able to boggle the mind thoroughly on the subject during a surprise clam call. Before we get to estimate the contentedness of clams, however, a few facts need to be established by him.

One of the bits of a clam is called the *umbo*. The Latin name for the giant clam is *Tridacnidae*, meaning three bites or mouthfuls. The biggest ones weigh half a tonne, and Australia is one of the few countries in the world that protects them (on the Barrier Reef). Elsewhere, due to feral fishing, they are 'decidedly on the skids', says Professor Lucas.

But are they suffused with a sense of well-being? Well, firstly, it's important to know that clams are special not just because of their size, but because they have algae actually inside their tissues, so they just take the photosynthesis into their bloodstreams. Cool, huh?

One further key to the happiness of clams may be that 'there's not a great amount of brain activity – they can see movements of light; if you wave at them or pass a shadow across the mantle they will close and seem to squirt a bit in the direction where it's coming from'. (In other words a clam may have decided recent woodchipping policy.)

This also would be the source of the rumours of divers getting trapped by the foot by a giant clam. 'It's very sad. They have a completely wrong image', says the Professor. 'In German you pronounce them "Murdermoossels". The big ones can't close that fast because they've got to push litres of water out.'

But can he confirm or deny the collective euphoria in the clam world? 'Without being a clam you can't really say . . . to me it's a happy sight looking at all the clams with their mantles expanded. They're fine-looking animals.'

Oh, cut to the chase: are they happy? Are they what. Get this: 'They're very fecund. The big ones are the most fecund animals in the world. At one spawning we've counted one thousand million eggs . . . they are complete hermaphrodites: not even tidy hermaphrodites . . . a gonad the size of a football, that's completely (sexually) mixed . . .

'When they're stimulated, they release a great cloud of sperm into the water, then an hour or so later they may become sort of female and release their eggs, by and large not aiming to self-fertilise: they've got to hope there's a nearby clam . . . which fires up as well . . . if they detect eggs they can fire off sperm within a couple of minutes.' (Get that look off your face, Josephine.)

Well, as you can see, Professor Lucas is a bit of a smooth talker for a guy who has stimulated giant clams and then held out a jar to collect whatever comes out next. But to return, somewhat distracted, to the subject at hand: it makes me feel better to think that the clams are happy.

Sadly, Professor Lucas has moved on to studying pearl oysters, but there is still a special place in his heart for clams. When you think of Australia having somebody like that who could talk about big ones at the Zoology Olympics and go gold, gold, gold for Australia, it just makes you feel all proud and emotional and, well, as felicitous as a tridacnidae.

Sex and Possibly Romance

Snoring

'It's raining, it's pouring, the old man is snoring. He bumped his head on the end of the bed, and couldn't get up in the morning.' Well, I rather think it very likely that somebody else banged her old man's head on the bed, don't you? Perhaps this is what they mean when doctors say that snoring is not good for you.

Let's be frank. I have spent time next to many snorers. And not just the way you're thinking. Sometimes I have been in a crowded train, cinema or theatre. I have always admired those people who can just nap away at any time. Especially those bizarre people for whom sleep is a reaction to stress. 'This is a hijack! Everybody down on the floor or I'll shoot you! Wake up, you bastards!'

I can remember nap time at kindergarten. By the time I'd found the right mat, I'd lie there wondering how long it was until glass of Milo time and what the stain was on the ceiling in the shape of a giant bunny rabbit? Even then some kids snored.

A new book about snoring by Mark Ragg is optimistically called *Silent Night*. For many people, the snorees, as opposed to the snorers, the experience is more like *Sullen Night*. The book is full of the health reasons why you should try to fix a snoring problem, with lots of explanations of what the epiglottis does and what the uvula is – and I tell you what it sounds sexier than it looks.

The graph of normal sleep patterns throughout the night looks like the outline of a Manhattan skyline. Up and down, as my old uncle used to say, like a toilet seat at a mixed party. We have several periods of Rapid Eye Movement (REM) sleep during the average night, which goes to show that most of us can look shifty even when we're unconscious.

At one week old, Mr Ragg tells us, we have an average sleep of sixteen and a half hours. By adult life we usually settle for seven to seven and a half. I have to admit to being a variation. (If I don't get about nine hours on average I start biting the furniture and speaking to my loved ones through a megaphone from the roofs of nearby buildings. 'Would you like a cup of tea?' they signal, semaphorically. 'You and whose bloody army?!' I reply, sending down a hail of chokoes in a ballistic fashion.)

The book tells us that Albert Einstein slept only four hours a night. From the photos I think he slept in his suit and never brushed his hair, but you have to make allowances for people who invent theories that lead to the atomic bomb, if you're prudent.

I learned a lot about snoring from this book, including that getting drunk relaxes the pharynx (and getting really drunk probably makes the pharynx tell unlikely stories about its sexual conquests). As soon as I can locate the pharynx I'm going to have a stern word with it.

Some doctors think that snoring gives you nightmares, although not as much as drinking saki, watching 'Baywatch', and sleeping in the wardrobe. Anyway, cures for snoring range from surgery to sewing a tennis ball into the back of your jarmies so you don't sleep on your back – although this presupposes that you are a pyjama-wearing tennis-playing snorer.

Luckily, I have finally found a sleeping partner who does not snore. No, the mighty Des Tiny, wiglet-maker to the middle class and *bon vivant*, is far more likely to thrash about in his terry-towelling velour shorty pyjama ensemble, laughing wildly in his sleep, tearing off his wimple and shouting 'Lucretia! Phyllida! Minxes all! To the battlements, and don't spare the negligees!' while accompanying himself on small whinnying noises and languid bicycular movements. I think it's time he learned how to snore.

Great Expectations

According to some toady called Andrew Morton, friends of the Princess of Wales say she is 'absolutely hell-bent' on finding another man. This other man will be 'clean cut, lean and rangy, well spoken, courteous, and with a wry sense of humour'.

This seems to be prohibitively specific. I mean, say the Princess of Wales is sitting on the tube one day, reading a copy of *Vogue*'s latest Trout Fishing Boots issue, and a clean-cut, lean and rangy, courteous and wryly amusing chap sits next to her, saying, 'Oy! Is this seat taken, or what?'.

In that moment, the Princess's hopes will be dashed awkward. If, however, she had told her tittle-tattling friends, 'I'm interested in anything with trousers and an XY chromosome configuration type thing, yah', then there's nowhere to go but up. The rest of his qualities would be a bonus, rather than a prerequisite.

There will be teams of photographers trying to catch Di's new squeeze with a three-day growth and a vodka hangover dressed in jarmie bottoms with little green cars on them. Journalists trying to fatten him up. Childhood

Sex and Possibly Romance

enemies produced to testify that once, when a Besser brick fell on his head, he used fairly discourteous language. Former girlfriends to insist that he's as funny as a Kevin Bloody Wilson song. And editorial teams trying to work out what the hell 'rangy' is. The guy, like Di's expectations, has nowhere to go but down.

Mademoiselle magazine is wading into the requirements debate, announcing its latest cover story 'How to Find a Man Who'll Really Love You. Nice Guys Do Exist!'. Well, der. Although somewhat disconcertingly, the article is written by somebody called Skip Hollandworth, who you'd reckon would have a vested interest in the question. Skip's contention, if somebody called Skip could be said to have contentions, is that girls always go for bad guys.

I guess the kind of guy Skip is referring to is the kind of guy with an elaborate record for grievous bodily harm, or maybe the sort who says, 'I don't want to have sex with you but maybe we could go to bed and see what happens. What was your name again? How about a foot massage? Help me, I have no Plan C.' Or the kind of guy who has ever won the Humpty Doo pub drinker of the month award. For example, one of the winners of this prestigious Northern Territory award in the 1980s was called Animal. Mr Animal's contention was that he liked XXXX beer best because it was like 'angels pissing on yer tonsils'.

Personally, I don't think women always go for these guys: it's hard to imagine Mr Animal getting much of a look in with the Princess of Wales, although at this stage I think it's best not to actually rule anything out.

Undeniably, sometimes women go for the bad guys. This is partly because bad guys are said to be more interesting, and partly because the women have lost their minds. This drives nice guys crazy, according to Skip, because they wonder why they're not attracting the girls, as it couldn't possibly be that they are not interesting.

Whereas, if you ask some women, they'll tell you that all the nice guys already have girlfriends and all they are left with is the choice between Mr Animal, an alien abduction, or Skip, who pleads, 'Why not have [a relationship] with a guy who's good for you and good to you? Isn't that what you've always wanted?'.

Nah. What we've always wanted is a bespectacled, passionately tender and brainy Glaswegian percussionist with neat sideburns, a good line in Hawaiian shirts, a passion for James Lee Burke books, a red heeler, a ute, a wildly ludicrous sense of humour and, oh, maybe a beach house, and who is not attractive to other women. Also, he should shower.

Mothers-in-Law

A British health magazine (an oxymoron, surely?) has proposed that men should check out their prospective mother-in-law as a guide to what their wife might look like in later years – and concluded that a man should scarper if his mother-in-law isn't babe material.

'If you can detect traces of something you fancy there, well and good', says *Men's Health*. 'But if she looks like a vast melted waxwork with her bulk cushioned on two five-stone buttocks, get the hell out.' *Men's Health* explains how a woman might come to look like her mother: 'Feed her the same foods, extract from her the same number of children and thirty years from now this could be what you wake up next to'.

Perhaps this is what the English mean by 'breeding' – it sounds like advice cobbled from a greyhound training manual. 'Extract from her the same number of children' – you dreamy-eyed romantics at *Men's Health*, you. Shame it betrays an absolute ignorance of genetics. A woman, even if the same food is poked into her cage every day and the correct number of children extracted (perhaps there's a tally board in the front hall), may well end up looking like

Barbara Cartland, Aunty Glenda, Uncle Evelyn, the labrador or the third footman, or a mixture of all of them.

The advice was contained in an article advising on how to stay together, including doing some housework, and, MY FAVOURITE PART, beware of free-spirited women who like to dance on tables. Was the article written by Prince Andrew, or what? Who in their right mind would steer clear of a woman who spontaneously liked a good fandango among the fish knives? (Perhaps the answer is that some men prefer to pay for their table-top dancing.) And what of free-spirited women who have given up table dancing for chandelier-swinging, yodelling and biting members of the Queensland National Party?

I was unable to get a copy of the actual article before the presses rolled, rattled and hummed, but I wonder whether it mentioned that, as a statistical rule, women's health is better off if they never marry at all. And there seems to be no suggestion that a man nobly should remove himself from the running if his dad looks like something out of *Escape from the Planet Zorg* in order to save his wife's sensibilities in later years.

It reminds me of the advice of my friend Ginger Owen-Beeswax, who says you should always beware of men who don't like their mothers. Even if there is a good reason for them not to like their mothers, e.g. their mothers sent them to the milk bar for a packet of smokes in 1972 and then got in a cab to the airport, it will not augur well for harmoniousness in general, she believes. Another pal, Lucretia Flingform, dispenses with chaps in the romantic sense, although she insists it's because of personal sexuality rather than a disappointing squizz at male senior citizens.

If a mother-in-law or father-in-law is to be considered I would have thought there might be more important things to consider. Do they stuff the children with red food colouring and work them into a pre-bedtime frenzy? Does she arrive with white gloves and run her finger down the mantelpiece, making a face like Andrew Peacock? Or will she write you a public letter saying you should divorce as quickly as possible, like the Queen? Does he insist on coming round to mow your front lawn in his Y-fronts? Do they like your tattoos?

With the certainty of a frocked-up epigrammist before a fall, Oscar Wilde said, 'All women become like their mothers. That is their tragedy. No man does. That's his'.

I have my own thoughts on the matter. Never marry a man who is scrutinising your mother's buttocks.

3
Ads and Other Fat Fibs

You Beauty Industry Seminar

Gather round for a briefing, people. New campaign for 'cellulite control complex' cream — Dior's Svelte. Target market: women with fat on their thighs — that's 99 per cent of healthy grown women. Don't call it normal fat whatever you do, and certainly not cute. Bad cellulite, naughty cellulite.

The Svelte ad's got a close-cropped picture of a person with a wafty pink scarf around the midriff. Any questions? Magazine writer with her claw up in the front row, Chanel suit. By the way, beauty editors — well done on the free plugs.

Good question. I personally think it's an eight year old. If it's a grown woman I don't think she's eaten more than one baby carrot since 1989. Or the image might be computer-generated. I don't think we care. The ad's just there to make normal-sized women feel like dirty great heffalumps.

I'm glad you pointed that out, Anoushka. Yes, some 'thigh creams' have run foul of the Trade Practices Commission. But none of the Dior ads claim that your thighs actually get thinner. Because if they did the product would have to be registered under the Therapeutic Goods Act and evidence would have to be presented as to how it changes the body. So the ads talk about changing 'the appearance'. (And not about the price: $69 for a 4–8 week supply, 200 millilitres.)

> *If in doubt, refer to the ads and be brief about what's IN the stuff ('an exclusive concentrate of plant extracts' will do) or what it does ('an unprecedented effectiveness tested under scientific control' is fine).*

This week I rang two city department store Dior counters anonymously and asked how Svelte worked. 'It works on the bottom layer of the skin', said one. 'Helps to eliminate fat — cellulite I should say — from the body... great results.'

The other saleswoman was even more effusive. 'Ooh, cell rejuvenation. Europe's leading, number one product. Stimulates blood circulation, we're launching it today in the store. Lymphatic; stimulates the lymph glands... breaks down the cellulite orange peel look, breaks down the lymph [sic] system, it stimulates the blood... Fantastic.'

Dr Greg Crosland, spokesman for the Australasian College of Dermatologists, is confused by these claims, probably because he just can't *match* that superior training and medical knowledge of a part-time cosmetics sales assistant. 'Works on the bottom layer of the skin? What on earth does that mean?... Does she mean the dermis? [And] if you're rubbing it on a fatty bum you're nowhere near a lymph gland... There are no lymph glands in the area... and if you "break down the lymphatic system" you get lymphoedema.' I explain that I presume she was referring to the evergreen claim that the lymphatic system can 'eliminate toxins' that cause cellulite. 'I doubt that toxins have anything to do with cellulite', he said.

Cellulite, Dr Crosland says, is the normal dimpling effect caused by the tethering to the skin of fatty tissues, which are contained in a honeycombed fibrous tissue network. That network becomes less strong through gravity, ageing and sun damage. The man has no sense of marketing!

'I'd like to see the substance of the "scientific" claims, whether it was a double blind, data and so on', he said. Fat chance. 'I would be very sceptical about the claims', says Dr Crosland. Ha! What a party pooper! I doubt he'll be quoted much in the beauty pages!

So get out there, people, make 'em feel bad about their standard dimply bits and sell, sell, sell! There's money in them thar jars of gloop. Remember, when it comes to cosmetics companies: beauty is in the eye of the stockholders!

The Hydration of Firmly-Sue

Intrigued mightily by the woman in the L'Oreal telly ad who demonstrates how a face cream makes her skin 54 per cent more smooth and 71 per cent more radiant, we broke into L'Oreal's heavily guarded Institut du Babedom HQ and stole her telephone number. What follows is the *exclusif* interview *avec* the severely hydrated Firmly-Sue Glamoursquared, 87, of Wichita.

Firmly-Sue enjoyed her three days in Florida Keys shooting the ad, but is happy to be home, where she conducts eyebrow awareness workshops in the off season and consults on whether wearing yellow makes blonde people look like a dead daffodil.

Did you enjoy making the ad? 'I especially like it when I hold the wafer-thin mobile phone to my ear and don't say anything', confided Firmly-Sue. 'Of course, keen students of lipreading can tell that in the shot where I'm surrounded by attentive men in suits, I do say "Wa".'

Firmly-Sue's rise to cheekbone prominence hasn't been easy. 'Once durin' a shoot the bulldog clip on the back of my head flew off. They didn't get the tension right, that day, no sir', she chuckles girlishly. 'One of my jowls flapped forward and concussed one of the make-up team managers. How we roared!'

Any other problems? 'Well when they show how the sunscreen works, and they filmed all those little bitty arrows bouncing off ma haid, it really smarted! But of course it's all part of the warp in life's rich tapestry.

'And, of course, it's tough having to get strapped to the Glowometer three times a day to have my radiance tested. One day it was only 37.897 per cent improved. If I was allowed to have facial expressions I would have sobbed myself to sleep that day. And, of course, the smoothness test is the most difficult. After they drag you through the hedge with the front-end loader and measure the flange factor against the wind resistance on the dermis wibbling, a girl needs a hearty meal, such as a snow pea.

'Although heavens to goodness, I need to watch my weight! Last winter I let myself go and simply balloooooned up to a size 4 (Australian size 2)! Luckily my modelling agent shot me in the leg and that brought me up short.'

We must compliment you on that obedient, shiny hair. 'I should think it would be right shiny', she said modestly. 'Those varnish technicians could get plumb 'ornery otherwise. Diggity, the advances in technology are plumb amazing. One Thursday, my hair was 17.9474837 per cent shinier than it was at 5.14 p.m. the previous Tuesday. I wish somebody had noticed', she sighed wistfully, yet bravely.

And tell us, Firmly-Sue, those fabulous faded-denim coloured eyes you had in the ad: coloured contact lenses? 'Why the very idea! No, we borrowed those from Christopher Walken for the day. He was between movies and glad of the cash.'

And that so-practical pale beige suit in the ad, in which you ponce around looking vacant, and as if somebody slapped you on the back of the head your face would twang off into the middle distance? What is the woman you portray actually doing? 'Doing, honey?' said a puzzled Firmly-Sue. 'I don't rightly see where that comes into it.'

Is the woman in the ad a stockbroker, an architect, an interior designer? 'Y'know, come to think on it, if some gal is going to know that they're 71 per cent more radiant, she'd probably be real happy about higher mathematics. I reckons as she might be involved in testing the string theory of physics.'

Warning: this column is now 43 per cent more truthful than when it started.

The Adulation of the Anorexi

There's a film on at the moment called *Farinelli*, about an eighteenth-century soprano opera singer, one of the many boys castrated so they would maintain their high voices. Parents of the promising prepubescent singers were paid, and the children were taken away and trained, usually in a religious institution.

This, clearly, was not a brilliant idea. No matter how good a singer a bloke is going to be it seems a bit much to deprive him of his precious cobblers at a tender age. Sure, he could make that decision himself at eighteen, but you might want to rope him to a pontoon in the middle of the Irish Sea until he came to his senses and decided to be a guitarist instead.

I was thinking about the castrati, the mention of whom makes any fella cross his legs and say 'Oooooh', because of the girls as young as six who are training to be Olympic gymnasts all over Australia. When I was researching a book about body image, I came across the quotes of a former gymnast who now coaches young Australian girls. She said she didn't go through puberty until she was eighteen. She explained that when she stopped training,

Ads and Other Fat Fibs 53

she grew almost 30 centimetres in three months. I do not find this a charming role model story. It makes me want to go, 'Aaaaarggghhhh'.

Ask any woman who has escaped the clutches of childhood ballet or high-level gymnastics about the legacy. They still feel the humiliating comments about their shape. Some of them still shriek at the sight of a Salada and run into the distance to avoid anything that approaches the concept of lunch. The causes and treatments of eating disorders are individually varied. But some conclusions can be drawn, and here they are.

It is not a brilliant idea to set young girls goals of perfection or to get them to weigh themselves a lot or make negative comments about their bodies. It's a tad spooky to punish them for putting on 0.01 of a kilogram, as has been alleged happens to some gymnasts in training.

It may be that telling girls they should look like thistledown but throw themselves around like dervishes could result in serious weirdness and injury. It's entirely possible that imparting the concept of hunger as a friend could have weeny repercussions later in life.

It would be fairly unfabulous to teach young girls that getting natural fat deposits around their chests, hips and thighs – growing up – is a tragedy for their career. It might be kind of weird to limit their body fat level artificially so that they cannot menstruate.

It would be pretty much unhelpful to teach them that they could 'lose' weight by sweating it off in a sauna, as has also been alleged. It wouldn't be exactly wonderful for them to feel that they let their coaches, parents, team mates and the entire country down if they look fondly upon a scone.

If this is what is happening, we must take advantage of it immediately. Let's introduce eating disorders as an Olympic sport and be in a good position to hang the gold medal around some fragile baby-bird-like necks come the year 2000. Instead of the castrati, we could call them the anorexi.

We could have bulimic-cam in the toilets, and find sponsors among the psychiatric institutions. Instead of drug tests, the competitors could be banned for having evidence of food in their system. Or hips. You've got to break a few eggs to make an omelette, if that's not too close to the terrifying concept of breakfast.

Men: Hold on to Your Willy

Look out, boys! Lock the doors and arm yourselves with semi-automatic confidence: the Body Police have a new hit squad in town. Hard-sell advertisements for hard bodies are bursting forth like Chesty Bond's chin. They're talking 'body-sculpting cosmetic surgery'. They're talking 'rejuvenation'. They're talking trash.

They want your body. They want to cut, slice and splice your face. They want to break your nose and then force it into another shape (without any football involvement). They want to put metal tubes in your gorgeous soft bits and lever them around with brute force until they break down the cells inside and suck 'em out. They also want to get their hands on your willy. And what they want to do with your willy doesn't bear thinking about. (Suffice to say it may involve a fat transplant from your stomach.) You can also get pectoral and calf implants if you want a drinks tray on the back of your leg and breasts like a Barbie doll.

Be warned, the pressure is starting in on you in earnest: impossibly proportioned blokes in ads for moisturisers, undies, aftershave, sports drinks and hair 'replacement'.

With the benefit of years of being told we're hideous, take a tip from us here on Planet Girl.

These joints only thrive in an atmosphere of insecurity and misplaced envy. They need you to believe that your normal splendid self is somehow freakish. They'll pick on exactly the things that many blokes have to maximise clientele: hair loss, plump bits and character lines. The men in the ads will be young professional models who do gym exercises for hours a day. Their hair is carefully jooshed. Their teeth are whitened by computer 'enhancement'. Their photographers have spent years working out the best angles and lighting. (These models are kept in a compound in Los Angeles and only allowed out in the company of a trained stylist.)

According to several sources, many male cosmetic surgery clients are married to cosmetically altered women. Do they promise to love, honour and obey, as long as you both shall look like a catalogue model? ('Darling! Here in this radiant moonlight, you look . . . operable.')

One 'aesthetic surgery' chain claims, 'All in the aim for better self-image and greater self-esteem, cosmetic surgery has a lot to offer the "average male"'. It says that penis enlargement is only performed after 'expert counselling and evaluation'. I'm absolutely sure it doesn't happen like this but I can't help imagining a white-coated Dr Schwarzenegger saying, 'Jeez, mate, that's a weeny one. I counsel you to give us a lot of money'. (Do independent willy-evaluators offer a second opinion? 'No worries with that one, sailor. You could do a lot with one of those.')

Ads and Other Fat Fibs 57

Ads for cosmetic surgery don't talk about other ways of boosting self-esteem, or mention risk: that's assessed by the surgeon and the anaesthetist. According to Dr Mike Martyn, from the Australian and New Zealand College of Anaesthetists, there is a risk of death for roughly one in 100,000 healthy patients who are anaesthetised. There are also run-of-the-mill risks and side-effects during or after a procedure that can include temporarily impaired mental faculties, nerve damage, hypothermia or overheating and, let us not underestimate it, pain and recovery. All of these side-effects can be minimised by a good anaesthetist. But why risk it for a non-medical reason?

We girlies have been targeted for so long that sometimes we think we look like mummified dugongs. So don't you start. Let's make a deal, fellas – if you don't expect us to look like a 'Baywatch' extra on Prozac, we won't expect you to look like a brain-dead, moulded lump of Bakelite. Works for me.

What New Woman?

I went searching for a new idea in *New Idea* magazine. A reader complained to the beauty tips column, 'I had my nose fixed last year and am unhappy with the result because it now has a lump on one side and looks lopsided. I am having my breasts enlarged in a few months and wonder if I could have my nose fixed at the same time?'.

Now, does the advice columnist say, 'Good lord, woman, quit while you're ahead'? Or, 'I hope you're not going back to the person who botched your hooter'? Or even, 'Look out you don't end up with nostrils on your nipples this time'?

No, she advises breezily: 'It sounds as if you have already consulted a surgeon about the breast operation, so why not ask him about having both operations at once?'. Well, why not get a head transplant and a full bottom removal while you're at it? Who ARE these people?

So then I went looking for a new woman in *New Woman* magazine. *New Woman* used to run ads with a photograph of a pear – a reference to the natural shape of most women. Its latest ad has the 'hips' sliced off the pear, to promote a 'guide' to cosmetic surgery in the March issue described as 'politically correct', whatever that means. Emblazoned on the cover is: 'Lift, Enhance, Improve'.

One part concludes, 'And when all else fails, when it becomes apparent that a surgeon is our only saviour, ensure we make an informed decision'. If only cosmetic surgeons would grow a beard, put vanity licence plates saying MESSIAH on the Porsches and adjust the wattage on their haloes so we can spot them easily. Luckily *New Woman* includes a price list of cosmetic surgery procedures (using a Barbie doll for illustration) and some handy phone numbers.

Nowhere in the section is a full list of possible side-effects, or an examination of the reasons for wanting to change your appearance or any alternatives such as counselling, focusing on other areas of life, a body image discussion group or a damned good lie down. It does point out that surgery might not make you happier, although it's been peachy as anything for two pals of the editors', apparently.

There's another page of celebrity bosoms and bits headed 'Get a Lift'. Then pages of free plugs for cosmetics and non-scalpel 'treatments' for the 'fainthearted'. These include a 'handheld instrument with a round 24-carat gold-tip applicator that uses thermic stimulations to give the skin a firmer, fresher appearance' ($200) and a 'seaweed extract powder' ($78 a month) that is 'believed to trigger the skin's own repair system'. Believed by whom it is not said. Possibly a deranged beauty product junkie called Candy who thinks alien abduction cured her rough, dry elbows.

An author is quoted who thinks breast massage will impart a full and youthful appearance to the breasts (I imagine going the grope on your earlobes will make them look positively prepubescent); there's an anti-surgery quote from Germaine Greer and an endorsement from Patsy and Edina of 'Absolutely Fabulous'. The article on laser surgery to burn away character lines does say that anyone with a day surgery licence is allowed to use lasers in Australia, but it does not mention that in the hands of the less qualified, some lasered patients have been SET ON FIRE, sweetie.

Other stories in this *New Woman* include 'Can You Be Too Independent?', why Sharon Stone can't find love (although it turns out she has a boyfriend), and 'How to Get on with People You Loathe'. If anybody wants me I'll be in the broom cupboard, waiting until there's a magazine called *Old Woman*. Would somebody please poke a Tim Tam under the door every seven minutes? Thank you.

Get a Loada the Cars on Miss Venezuela

Have you seen the front of *Mode* magazine this month? The model's legs don't exactly go on forever but they'll get you halfway to the Big Pineapple. *Mode*'s cover notes say 'Achieve Yasmeen Ghauri's Look Using Make-up by Lancaster'. (It is not explained how make-up, however artful, gives the impression that you are 7 metres tall and have left your hips in the cutlery drawer.)

So I rang *Mode*'s editor to check on the extent of the computer photo-doctoring. Were Yasmeen's hips 'trimmed' as well as her legs lengthened? Not guilty, said Maggie Alderson, unless the image was altered at its source overseas. 'I think this picture is a combination of the camera angle and her physique . . . she's a freak', Ms Alderson said. 'She just has the most unbelievable legs. She's not perfect: she's got cellulite at the back.'

This is most disquieting. Just when you think you've got a handle on the world as completely falsified, something turns out to be realish. Nothing is what it really seems. When a picture that looks digitally manipulated turns out to be maybe a plain old photograph after hours of make-up, expert lighting, big posing and some surgical gauze over the lens, I just don't know WHAT to believe any more.

Some magazines already use computer manipulation of images, but it's time to make it compulsory so that, you know, we know that we don't know what we know any more. Why, then we'd all know where we are. We could have a good lie down because we know where we stand.

We've got the technology, let's use it. Let's dispense with the cover line on the current issue of the magazine called *Men's Stuff*, which actually says 'How Feminism Can Help You Get Laid'. Let's have digitally enhanced Y-fronts instead. (That's not really how you get some action. You get some action by being breathily involved in a mutual attraction, or by being good at it, or by having a come-hither wink, or by knowing how to pronounce the word 'condom', or by refraining from saying 'my wife doesn't understand me', or by asking nicely. It is also possible to 'get laid' if your partner is insensibly drunk, or being paid for it. Or sometimes pouting will help. This is a complex matter: honestly, you'd think these men's magazines would be more thorough in their advice, but I'm on a tangent here.)

With this new computer technology in photograph manipulation Yasmeen's legs can go on to Cape York. We can have waists far too small to fit in the essential internal organs of a real person. We can have way, way big cars, breasts the size of Miss Venezuela, Miss Venezuelas the size of cars, cars shaped like . . . oh, never mind.

Football magazines can have digitally invented high marks or bizarre tackles. We can have politicians in compromising positions with domestic animals, or, for the election campaign pamphlets, a manipulated image that looks for all the world as if a politician and his family are in the same room together (maybe that's stretching credulity a little too far).

When you get your family snaps back from Kodak you could find out that you're 3 metres taller than your brothers, the Holden bonnet is the size of an aircraft carrier, Aunty Daphne's lost 67 kilos, everyone's teeth look like they've been Liquid Papered, your Dad looks exactly like Yasmeen without the cellulite, your caravan's turned into a holiday house in Broome and the dog looks like Gary Sweet. Actually the dog probably does look like Gary Sweet. Basset hound eyes and all over the bloody newspaper the minute you let your guard down.

A Cracked Force

In Australian History we learned of the Eureka Stockade, something about a whole heap of rebel miners who didn't want to be brutally oppressed any more so they built a fortress at the Ballarat goldfields but got thrashed by the government troops anyway. That's about all I can remember. (I think Sigrid Thornton was in it.)

Anyway, now this joint is a big tourist attraction called Sovereign Hill – a historical tourist precinct with replica buildings, horse-drawn thingies and paid extras poncing around in period costumes (you can still get the skirts at Country Road). I know this because my parents took me there once and we pretended to 'pan for gold' except really you only got sunburn.

A recent ad seeking tourist visitors to Sovereign Hill is far more enticing. 'New York Is Not the Only Place Kids Play with Guns', says the headline. (Ha, ha! The fun fact that children regularly maim and kill each other in New York, deliberately or by accident, is a brilliant marketing angle hitherto overlooked.) A photo shows two grown men dressed in toy soldier uniforms and a small child with an upside-down black bucket on his head. The men have antique rifles; the child has a wooden cut-out rifle.

Let us take the rest of the advertisement line by line: **'Admittedly they're only wooden rifles'**. If they were really serious about it, the kids would be bullied into drug gangs and given semi-automatic weapons for drive-by shootings, mobile phones, and no futures. Half measures will only ensure that people take their holidays in a more authentic environment with relaxed gun laws, say South Central Los Angeles or East Timor.

'But absolutely everything else at Sovereign Hill is authentic.' That's more like it! Goldfield anarchy with no running water, no sewerage system, calico tents with sloppy mud floors, scurvy, racism against the Chinese gold-diggers, an ill-managed rabble of armed young hoons let loose in military uniforms, desperate binge-drinking in town and rampant syphilis, dysentery and tuberculosis! Hurrah!

'And during January, the kids can join up as real redcoat soldiers for half an hour of serious training.' Frankly, half an hour doesn't seem enough. Not if they have to learn to collect the rum ration, abuse the populace and find out how to shoot to kill and reload in the dark. They'll need to learn advanced bayoneting, and rudimentary ways of bandaging gangrenous buckshot injuries. I'd say three-quarters of an hour ought to do it before they're released back into the community with the idea that going around with an imitation gun and shouting 'BANG!' at people is a fab idea.

And obviously, it's no good training a crack force of hysterical youngsters to be the suppressing forces if you don't get a whole lot of other kids to be the oppressed. Clearly all the smaller, weaker kids who aren't good at games or have less money to pay for training should be rounded up inside the complex and forced to play the part of the gold-diggers.

These cherubs could be herded to the top of the hill for the purposes of being bashed right up at hourly intervals. At the end of the day they would be able to meet their parents in the Burgers'n'Counselling Pavilion. (Parents can spend the afternoon in the Ye Olde Dum-Dum Bullet Saloon.)

'They'll be dressed in all the gear and taught to drill up and down the Main Street.' That'll come in handy. Kids *will* play soldiers of course, the trick is to formalise the whole show and get their parents to pay for it. Might be a good idea to put in for a government grant and call them Junior Conflict Resolution Seminars. Wooden weapons are a good start: it's about time we recognised the right of toddlers to bear arms.

It's been a smashing success in New York.

A Short History of Excuses, Excuses

An emperor called Nero when asked why he didn't defend Rome when it was sacked (or as we say these days, 'downsized'), or burned ('ripped off bad'), replied, 'Wasn't my fault. I was having a violin lesson'.

After the Three Mile Island nuclear power plant went ballistic and started to melt down in 1979, the nuclear industry blamed media 'sensationalism' for upsetting people.

In the 1980s 'Spycatcher' case, a frightfully senior English civil servant told an Australian court that rather than telling big fat porkies about British Intelligence services, he had simply 'been economical with the truth'.

When former opposition leader Alexander Downer's joke about domestic violence policy being called 'The Things that Batter' went over like a tonne of bricks, he initially blamed people who didn't have his sense of humour.

But the Princess of Wales has beaten them all for classic excuses in saying recently that she does not have 'cellulite' – the perfectly natural dimples that almost every grown woman, regardless of size, has on her upper leggie bits. The Princess claimed that shadows photographed on her legs were caused by the imprint from the pattern of a leather car seat. (This is perfectly feasible. It is a known fact that being tied to a rattan cane lounge suite for a considerable length of time while in the nuddy causes the skin to take on every appearance that it has been knitted in the dark by an Aran-jumper-fixated cable-stitch fancier.)

If her tactics catch on, we'll all end up apologising and inventing desperate, Di-like excuses: 'No, no, NO! I haven't got any lines on my face! These creases are caused by pillow abuse and wind directional changes. And I haven't got an enormous bottom, either; I am carrying my shopping home inside a handy trouser-cavity. I do not have a convex tum-tum; I have been expecting triplets since 1989. Usually I look just like a young Joan Collins, it's just that I've lent my real face out for the day and this is my back-up, just-for-round-the-house face.

'Actually my legs are twice as long as this, but the lighting in here is very unflattering. It may seem like I have a humungous pimple on the end of my nose, but actually it is a maraschino cherry that accidentally became glued there during a cocktail party incident last Friday. (I still have a stuffed olive down my sock and a cheese vol-au-vent stuck to my Wonder Bra.) Several of you may have assumed that my hair is naturally oily, when in fact I ran my fingers through my hair, completely forgetting that I was in the process of stripping a left-handed carburettor and sprauncing the Big End clockwise near the manifold doobrey on a small touring car.'

Even Prince Charles might have to get in on it: 'The

Ads and Other Fat Fibs 69

analysis of the tabloid photograph that purports to be one's enormous ears will prove conclusively that there was a UFO passing behind one's head at the exact moment the original photograph was taken, giving it the appearance of big flappers. Plus, it may seem like one has a very small, weedy chest but, actually, one leaned against a venetian blind with wet paint on it giving the impression of visible ribs'.

We might do better to remember that the ancient Roman goddess of the moon and hunting, Diana, is often depicted in paintings and statuary with big, rippling thighs, hips to reckon with and a bow and arrow. This is considered more classically artistic and interesting than the image of a depressed ex-bulimic hounded by the Press and clutching a Chanel handbag full of credit cards and soggy tissues. Take it away, Nero.

4
Politicking

Shut Up about Political Correctness

When a Liberal Party adviser, commenting on the fact that there was only one Labor voter in an electorate, said last week that she didn't know the identity of the 'nigger in the woodpile', a reporter described this as politically incorrect. It wasn't politically incorrect. It was racist, it was thoughtless, it was just plain dumber than dumb.

A reviewer of a CD-ROM game claimed that because all the heroes in the game were female, this was 'in keeping with the politically correct 90s'. Well, how about 'refreshingly different, considering the 458 trillion sexist, violent games mostly available in the reactionary 90s', or 'astonishingly enough, this could be fun for girls'?

A football commentator thinks it's 'politically correct' to suggest that women could be commentators too. What if it's just a good idea? Or an interesting idea? Or makes good marketing sense for a TV channel interested in attracting more viewers? If he thinks women are more stupid than men, why doesn't he just say so? Oh, he does? That's not 'politically incorrect' (and therefore a bit naughty and thrilling), that's old-fashioned and kind of tedious.

A Canberra journalist assumes that some art lovers will think an exhibition of portraits of socialites and 'beautiful people' to be 'politically incorrect'. How about boring? How about fascinating? How about let people make up their own minds? How about read a dictionary and see if you can find some words that don't start with a 'p'?

A car reviewer described a new BMW as a 'politically correct compact that comes in under the $50,000 luxury tax level'. Oh, speak English why don't you? It was impossible to tell from the article exactly why this phenomenally expensive vehicle is 'politically correct' except perhaps because the cigarette lighter and ashtray are an optional extra, or because the car, I swear this is what he reckons, has a 'willingness to participate in events'. Say what?

A correspondent to a newspaper wants to know if a politician's use of the word 'myopic' as an insult is 'politically correct'. How about rude? Ineffective? How about 'less alarmingly obscene than his usual insults'?

Can't we have a moratorium on the phrase 'political correctness', punishable by cattle prod? It's just about the laziest form of insult I've ever heard. There's always a word or a phrase that could be substituted that would actually make sense, if that's not too radical a concept. I have been accused of political correctness because I don't drink coffee. For God's sake, I just don't like coffee, okay?

'Political correctness' is used with purse-lipped fervour by all those right-wing fogies who complain about any other import from America. 'Isn't it OUTRAGEOUS that those filthy, mindlessly slavish children wear their baseball caps backwards? They should all be flogged and forced to play silly mid-on, now there's an Australian sports tradition.' Yeah, right.

The phrase is used as an all-purpose, censoring insult. 'Girls should be able to wear trousers.' Ooooh, politically correct, shut right up. 'It's probably a good idea not to chop down every tree in the country.' Ooooh, politically correct, be embarrassed about your opinion. 'Maybe black people shouldn't be spat at in the street.' Ooooh, really politically correct, go to your room.

If this goes on they'll be making keyboards for journalists with a button for 'politically correct'. The very phrase is the Paterson's curse of our age, a flourishing, unnecessary imported nuisance. Not unlike Michael Bolton records. If language was a palette, any sentence with 'politically correct' in it would be beige. Whenever you feel the phrase leaping to your lips, stop it, or you'll go bland.

Shut Right Up

SHUT UP. Just shut up, everybody. That means you, Bill Hayden, former governor-general. Listen: I will PAY anybody who can a) shut Bill Hayden right up, and b) round up and ritually WHACK any journalists who review his recently released autobiography, quote his pathetic opinions, suggest that any of us might be in any way INTERESTED in tired old has-been up-themselves dill-brain bloody neo-conservative idiots who think nuclear weapons are a tickity-boo idea and, *unsolicited in any way*, crap on and ON about the size of Bob Hawke's private parts. We were not interested in *his* stupid dumb book and we are even less interested in *yours*, Mr Rose-to-the-rank-of-chief-bloody-fête-opener – so just SHUT UP.

Did I mention that I am giving up smoking?

And there's just a FEW THINGS I WANT TO GET OFF MY CHEST. Mostly my lungs, which are possibly at this very moment going to be coughed up. Actually I don't think I will cough up my lungs. It feels and sounds more like I am going to cough up a piano accordion made of phlegm. God, what a word. They made it that hard to spell to discourage people from thinking about it, let alone writing it down, but not me, no. HA HA. Phlegm, phlegm, phlegm. SHUT UP.

Listen to me, you fundamentalist Christians and weaselly so-called morals campaigners who are against people having sex without a permit from the Government ('marriage licence') and against gay people getting married and having children: SHUT UP. It's none of your business. Hey, I disapprove of YOU. I disapprove of you getting married and – hell's bells – reproducing. Yuk: that's disgusting. And if you must do it, why can't you just KEEP QUIET about it and stop shoving it down our throats with your revolting Christian Pride marches and your snide little letters to the editor: I DON'T WANT TO SEE THAT SORT OF FILTH IN THE MEDIA.

You and your appalling 'Family Values', which are no more than repressive rules with which to frighten children and everybody else. But do I claim you shouldn't be allowed to get married? Do I campaign against the deeply offensive Christian advertisements on the telly with IDIOTS SINGING? No. YOU PEOPLE MAKE ME SICK. You mean-spirited, boring bullies – you can't stand anybody else having a good time doing something you disapprove of. You are so intolerant I'd like to come around to your offensively neat houses kept by women who have nothing to do since all the kids left home but POLISH THE LIGHT BULBS because you won't let women go out of the goddamn HOUSE and I'd electrocute you ALL. Oh yes, live and let live, I say.

I don't approve of you having children – they scream

and throw up on public transport and you bring them to public places where they drive everybody crazy and as a taxpayer I'M FORCED TO CONTRIBUTE TO YOUR LITTLE MORAL CONSPIRACY OF CHILD-BEARING. OH YES I'm supposed to pay for their birth in a public hospital and child endowment and education and their training and, on Medicare, for their measles and methadone and even their therapy when they realise their whole LIFE is a sham because you have filled their heads with narrow-minded, racist, sexist, money-is-more-important-than-anything DRIVEL. But do I say you shouldn't be allowed to have children?

It isn't any of my business. Oh no, I'm just supposed to PAY for it. I mean, not that anybody else's lifestyle should be at all threatened by ME seeing I'm just BANKROLLING YOU FREELOADING ULTRA-CONSERVATIVE LOONIES, so go right ahead, insult my gay friends, sneer at me for being childless and godless. Call me a slut. Do whatever you like, it's a free country, apparently. JUST GIVE ME A BLOODY CIGARETTE. And SHUT UP.

Bazza You Legend

A few years ago I was a reporter based in Darwin, which new editors seemed to think was Frontierland. Mostly, this involved being rung up in the middle of the night by eager sub-editors saying, 'Apparently this guy, Bent-Hat McGoolicuddy, just beat off a 56-foot croc with a cocktail umbrella. Can you do us a snappy ten pars?'. To which I would reply 'Nope' and go back to bed.

But my favourite stories involved Barry Coulter, Deputy Chief Minister of the Northern Territory. Barry didn't so much make colourful quotes as pull whole Dulux catalogues out of his gullet. It was Barry who told an anthropology conference that what he knew about anthropology you could chisel on the back of an aspirin. As Conservation Minister he said he was a lover of erosion, because it made the Katherine Gorge.

And in 1989 it was Barry, then Minister for Mines and Energy, who offered to drink a glass of water from a retention pond at Ranger uranium mine to prove that it was safe water to release into the Magela Creek system, through Aboriginal communities in Kakadu National Park. The families living there daily use the water for drinking, washing and fishing, as they have done all their lives, as their ancestors did before them.

So anyway, a whole lot of reporters and Barry drove down to spooky old Ranger and Barry bent his elbow. He made the kind of face you make when you're trying not to make a face. I asked him what he thought this proved given that his molecular make-up differed somewhat from, say, fish. Barry did not answer me. (This was more polite than a press secretary of his party who in response to my first introductory 'Hello' on another occasion, had greeted me by saying, 'You're a southern socialist cunt'. Fancy, and I thought I was a Sagittarian.)

Anyway, it's happening again. This time, the NT Acting Minister for Mines and Energy, Fred Finch, has offered to drink a glass of water from the creek system after a new release into the Magela, to prove it is safe. Note that Mr Finch has not offered to drink from the proposed *source* of the release, Ranger's retention pond two, which is by all accounts much heavier stuff than in retention pond four (Barry's tipple).

Can't say I blame anyone queasy at the prospect of up to half a million cubic metres of contaminated uranium mine waste water in their daily water supply. But while the Northern Territory is happy to have 83-year-old Big Bill Neidji appear in books, videos and documentaries promoting the Territory as a tourist destination, his wishes as a traditional owner of the land downstream from ERA's mine are ignored.

He and his relatives have been forced to court. One of them commented dryly in a letter to the Prime Minister that Big Bill 'knows of no scientist or government representative who is dependent on land and its food source downstream . . . he speaks for his country, he speaks for his grandchildren and the families downstream. He asks you to act responsibly for what you should value most of all. Land and its people. Who in government will heed his words?'.

The Northern Territory has a lot of ministers. They can keep sending them down there one by one to drink a tumbler each of Ranger pond water, or in the case of Mr Finch, Ranger-Lite from the creek. It won't prove a thing except that they know enough about responsible mine management and good manners to chisel it on the back of an aspirin. With a crowbar.

Is That a Bermb in Your Pocket, Cheri?

Many of you may still be experiencing short, sharp feelings of discomfort in the buttockular region following the recent and statesmanlike decision of the suavely attractive French Government to blow up some more nuclear bombs underneath the tediously tranquil and shamefully idle Pacific Ocean.

(The ocean in question is named for the Latin word *pacificus*, meaning peace-making. In French, it means 'Mine's bigger than yours ka BOOM zut alors it is leaking all over my Chanel shoes let's do it in Muraroa next time Jacques ka BOOM ka BOOM ka BOOM ha ha ha ha ha'. Sadly, much is often lost in literal translation, and it is time we respected the cultural traditions of the French, e.g. complete rudeness.)

We cannot fathom the intricate scientific or diplomatic negotiations about these tests. Happily, our representative is Senator Gareth Evans, hurrah, who said Australia would protest, but the test arrangements were not as bad as they could have been. Now, you might think that Evans is just utterly pathetic.

But clearly you're wrong and he's right: it COULD be worse. The tests could be conducted by an unmedicated manic-depressive one-armed first-year explosives student called Plastics Bertrand who intends to nuclear-bomb any and all shippery, especially any with the word 'Rainbow' on the hull, each Thursday, barring choir practice.

(Incidentally, after writing of the Order of Australia being awarded to the Indonesian Foreign Minister, Mr Alatas, we have received a letter from a serving member of our defence forces who is now 'too ashamed' to wear his medal for Member in the Military Division of the Order of Australia. Mr Alatas' award was welcomed by Foreign Minister Evans, whose hobbies are listed in *Who's Who* as golf, tennis and football in which the losers are not usually shot.)

Now that the atoms have settled after the first reaction to France's inalienable right to go ka BOOM in places unadjacent to France, let us scrutinise the evidence. We see that the tests are conducted under stringent guidelines.

Rule One
If a colonial power feels the need to test something evil and unspeakably dangerous, it will do so as near to the homes of foreign black people as deemed possible by Operations. The only exception to this is when the tests are conducted *in* the homes of foreign black people (see: Bikini, Maralinga, Monte Bello islands, etc.).

Rule Two
The colonial power shall wheel in scientists to say it's safe.

(A lot of tommyrot has been spake regarding the dangers of radioactivity. The radioactivity caused by nuclear bombs detonated under porous rocks in the sea at Muraroa Atoll is not dangerous because it is French radiation.

To elucidate: French products, such as champagne, are superior, and on a related matter the French do not tell lies about their products. You only have to look at their cellulite cures and bust-firming creams, which are high-quality amounts of herbal fat with extraordinary powers of gorgeousification at approx $560 per 100 millilitres.)

Rule Three
If you are afraid of a European ground and air war, it would be sensible to test your bombs under a faraway tropical ocean, just in case any of the fighting is switched to the subterranean Pacific because of rain or bad light.

Rule Four
Shut Right Up.

Comrades, we have a tradition of defending the French! Our men lie on their soil, why shouldn't the French lie to us? Don't let this issue die like a dispensable leetle angel fish! If you wish to protest to insolent Greenpeace Australia about its intended disruption of the glorious march of progress in the Pacific, call its membership line on 1-800-815-151.

Feral Policymakers on the Loose

You may have noticed a news item during the week about a feral hairstylist in Holland who tells models he needs to practise cutting their hair for a competition. He then cuts the hair in the model's own home and goes away again. He doesn't do a good job, but the police can't charge him with that.

I suggest the Dutch start trying to educate their models about bescissored-stranger danger. I mean, a bloke comes up to you in the street and says, 'You are very attractive, miss. Can I come home with you and cut your hair? I have my own pinking shears'. Who among us would trill, 'Just a little off the top, whoever you are'? Not me sister, I had a poodle perm once and it still gives me the willies just thinking about it.

Dutch police have dubbed their man 'the maniac hairdresser'. This, surely, is a bit strong. A maniac hairdresser would be bringing back the Dolly Cut. A maniac hairdresser would take three hours and a razor blade to make you look dissipated and insouciant. A maniac hairdresser does not go lickity-split hithering, thithering and dithering with scissors through the streets of Emmen accosting models. That is an opportunist.

Which brings me to politics and as regular readers know I'm as loathe as the next person to question the ways of the Foreign Minister, Senator Gareth Evans, widely tipped as the next Indonesian ambassador. To Australia. No, that can't be right . . . ah, widely tipped as Secretary-General of the United Nations. (I met a wide person the other day and they tipped it like mad.)

In this way I can only recommend to you the very experienced journalisto-commentators who have given up their opinion pieces on Mr Evans' handling of a) the French administration blowing up whatever they feel like whenever they feel like it in the Pacific and b) the withdrawn appointment of an Indonesian general as ambassador to Australia. (You will recall that the general had described as 'quite proper' the Dili massacre, in which several people who went to a funeral in East Timor got shot by Indonesian soldiers. The general said recently that there was a 'misunderstanding' of the 'interpretation' of his statement.)

One big-time commentator reckoned, 'To be fair . . . no one quite anticipated the vehemence of the reaction in Australia [against the general's appointment]. Something of the hysteria that gripped the country following the resumption of French nuclear testing in the Pacific carried over into this issue. Poor old [general] . . .' Another well-known political opinion writer said, 'In conducting foreign affairs, domestic opinion is just one factor to be taken into account'. (The other factors to be taken into account, obviously, are wind direction, goat entrails and horoscopes.)

But if I may be so bold, even though I haven't lived in a Canberra suburb for millions of years and I don't get off-the-record terribly secret briefings from Very, Very Important Senior Advisers, and I've never played tennis with Kim Beazley, I have an opinion too. What has been happening out here is not hysteria. It is a deep feeling about fairness and bullying. It is about morality, as unfashionable as that may be in political discussion these days. If we pay the wages of the whole Foreign Affairs mob, the least they can do is convey what we wish, i.e. Dear Sirs, would you please be so kind as to stop taking potshots at the neighbours?

Here's a hint for the pollies and the commentators: next time, all you have to do is ask. Like, 'Can I come home and give you a haircut?' or 'Is it okay if the French pop some more unbelievable amounts of radiation in the ocean on our east coast?'. We'll give you a straight answer.

Taxing Time

Join in whenever you feel ready: *Ohhhh give me a home, where the auditors roam, and the receipts are all printed in ink of the most delicate lavender shades and not visible to the human eyeeeeee.*

Yes, it be tax time again, and as we drag out our shoe boxes full of old bills, all written in red ink visible to the human eye at distances up to 70 kilometres away, we would do well to advise the Federal Government exactly how we would like our taxes spent. And not spent.

Rightyo then.

Pro Ballet

None of my taxes, thank you, to be spent on any seething anorexia factory of bickering frou-frou-pants, the freakiest kingdom of them all, Pro Ballet. Not that I've got anything against talented, bickering, flouncing anorexics, I just don't particularly want to give them any money to encourage it.

If, however, the Government chooses to put money into Alternative Pro-Fatty Boombah ballet companies, where young girls are encouraged to lerv their natural shape, look after their toes, galumph around to their heart's content, abandon vomiting as a career move, realise that being lighter than thistledown and still able to hurtle about is not a sane ambition, and pop off at elevenses for some cakie things, the Government may splash my cash around in this department willy and in particular nilly.

(General tutu wearing should be encouraged as a matter of course.)

Pro Bad Poets
Mollusc III

Perhaps
the fiery,
drifting,
screamingly
textured poets
could get
Big Fat
Grants
A Lot
Then Not
No More, no more
And then slag off
the Australia Council
Just a Thought
(1995)

Pro Opera Company
(Translated from the original Aztec)

Woman with cowhorns on head: Don't want to outlaw oper-aaaaa.
Large man in baritoney waistcoat: Just don't want to pay for other people to go and seeeeeee . . . IT.
Townsfolk in palazzo: Have you clowns got any id-eee-yeee-ha how much these outfits cost?
Chorus: Yes but they are very speccy! Very, very speccy!
Stagehands: Shut up you stupid columnist or we'll lose our jobs!
Chorus: Shoop, shoop, doo waddy wah, big time.

Pro Politicians

Is it considered absolutely imperative to use some of my cheerfully imparted taxes to pay the salaries of politicians with well-modulated voices, flip-top toupees, expense acounts, rellies on the payroll and skellies in the closet? Also, some fairly violent ambivalence is felt on the subject of arms to Indonesia, rather than legs in Cambodia, given the land-mine situation vis-à-vis kiddies.

On the other hand, I wouldn't mind suggesting that some of my taxes get shunted in the following directions: hozzies, kindies, circuses and the sole parent's pension (for those coming off the pension last year, the median length of time on it was about a year).

School Curricula

Philosophy lessons for all, self-defence for girlies and anger management for boys and vice versa if they'd like. Contraception advice, and complementary help with which are the working ends of a baby, and what to do with them when you've got them. Maths, volleyball, advanced physics, how to make a decent pikelet, and so on.

Grants for Really Naughty Artists

The English artist who recently flashed her bum at a judge and said 'So you don't want to see my bottom again, Wiggy!' is the sort of thing we need more of here in the art department. The artist in question had already served six months in jail for writing 'Merry Christmas' on her buttocks and showing them to a High Court judge. (No doubt this came as a surprise to many English sex workers who regularly show their buttocks to members of the judiciary, and get £50 rather than six months. As those wacky supermodels say in the exercise videos: Work it out!)

The Real Australian History

Dear Kaz
I am a high school teacher, and the principal doesn't think we should teach students that Australia was 'invaded', as this would be divisive. We have been told to teach that Australia was peacefully settled. Would it be rude to ignore the directive?
Sir, Country High School.

This invasion notion just kowtows to the politically correct namby-pambies. (I don't know about you, but I just adore the words 'politically correct' and I'm going to use them as often as possible, sometimes several times in the same sentence, against anyone I disagree with. Politically correct, politically correct, nyah, nyah, nyah.)

We've got to get over this guilt thing. There's a bunch of massacred, ill and vilified people in your past or present? Don't look back, that's what I say. Anyway, that's not what really happened and if it was it wasn't our fault and if it was we don't have to fix it and if we don't have to fix it we don't have to say it happened. Let's use some rational academic thought please.

You can imagine how surprised I was to find that Aborigines think they got invaded, just because they don't recall sending out for English criminals. Especially when I was taught at school that Aborigines were pretty much all dead. They can't have it both ways. They can't all be dead AND try to participate in Australian life. It's time they stood on their own two feet and paid for their own early funerals.

Australian history has been established. What happened was, Captain Cook, who was heroic, and Sigrid Thornton came up the Murray River on an historical paddleboat and discovered Australia in 1788. Everyone knows that the American always gets the girl, so they came to an arrangement with Kirk Douglas in a sticky-on grey beard. (Ernie Dingo was offered a non-speaking role.)

The Crown (merrye ye olde Englande) then sent out a lot of convicts to Old Sydney Town including some Charles Dickens characters. There was a gold rush, during which there was rum and McArthur invented sheep, on whose back the country rode. If any black people got shot after that it was only because they didn't have enough guns.

Sometimes some people got lost, like Burke and Wills, who were heroic. It was a very hard, pioneering life, but people were ingenious, as they were at Gallipoli, when we turned to America because of the fall of Long Tan, although the Yanks killed Phar Lap, who was heroic, as well as getting all the girls, because they were overpaid, over here and overbearing. (We won the war.)

A lot of horseriding got done, especially by Ned Kelly, who was heroic, but there were some women, who had to do it side-saddle because they had long skirts, but were very supportive. Some Chinese people were at the goldfields. Rabbits were a problem. Sir Robert Menzies (heroic).

Before that there was an uncivilised race who have been entirely assimilated and are grateful for the advent of civilisation upon their tragic and quite old Stone Age culture because of the introduction of modern medicine, education, syphilis, smallpox, racial prejudice, the concept of real estate, the churches' attitude to women and sex, Tasmania, long skirts for horseriding, childstealing, unpaid domestic service and the British legal system.

It has been that way for exactly 200 years, which has always been the amount of time since peaceful settlement, for time in the memorial. I hope that has cleared things up. Mervyn, I believe it's time for my injection.

(The writer was educated in Australia.)

5
Spirituality and Other Dippiness

My Tiny Shoulder Is Frozen

Last week I had a frozen shoulder. It sounds like a sprauncey cocktail: 'A zucchini daiquiri, a Fluffy Poindexter, a Pink Lady, a jug of crème de menthe, a Frozen Shoulder and Two Fat Ferrets on a Foreign Minister, hold the pineapple metho, thanks, Mac'. But a frozen shoulder is that thingie you get when you can't turn your head to one side or, if you can, you can only do it with your whole body and you look like Lurch in the Addams Family.

So anyway, I was desperate to have somebody do something to my shoulder, and ended up in a local massagery with Martin whose sign claimed expertise in sports injuries and frozen shoulders. I realise now that I should have read on down the list to where it said 'Channelling Lessons with Zahkarna' and 'Harmonious Crystal Healing' and 'Reiki' (which is kind of like hands-on faith healing, without the healing).

It was established that I had been doing a lot of drawing and typing, and had been a bit stressed. 'Do you mind if I ask you what star sign you are?' said Martin. I believe it was at this moment I began to feel a bit squirgly in the

Spirituality and Other Dippiness

old tum-tum. 'Sagittarius', I said, not without mirth. 'Well.' He shook his head. 'I could understand it if you were a Virgo.' (He'd be Robinson Crusoe on that one, then.)

Anyway, blow me down and halfway to ancient Egypt if Martin didn't explain, while fixing my shoulder, what my problem was. The right shoulder was related to the *right*-hand side of the body (uh-huh), which is my masculine side. This is the side that deals with paying bills and career. I was much better on the left side of my body, which is the *feminine* side, where the shoulder thinks about things like relationships and feelings. 'Don't you think it might be because I'm right-handed?' I asked. Martin thought anything was possible in this wacky old world, but you could tell he was pretty sold on the masculine theory.

Which is weird, you know, because I didn't know that paying bills was blokey. I wish I had rung Telstra last week and said, 'Sorry. Feeling a bit girly. Won't be paying the phone bill'. Now I understand all those blokes who say, 'I don't know how I feel. Ask one of my shoulders'.

Martin wanted to know whether I had heard of Louise Hay. I glanced at his bookshelves, for enough time to see the names of authors Dale Carnegie, Shirley MacLaine and Louise Hay. Yes, I've heard of her. Many of her followers believe that all disease is caused by bad thoughts or personality, a really charming philosophy being squirted around by some very dippy naturopaths and masseurs who give sensible ones a bad name.

One herbalist tells me she went to a lecture years ago and the 'teacher' told his students that tuberculosis happened to people who were mean with money (you know, like Aboriginal children in remote areas). A friend's mother was told by her chiropractor that he could cure Alzheimer's disease.

Another person I went to see about my neck gave me a pamphlet called 'A Rationale for Hydration of the Body'. A good rationale might be 'because otherwise you'll die' but this was not the point of the pamphlet, which contained a quote from Lyall Watson, *The Water Planet*: 'The fluid in our bodies is a perfect replica of that ocean in which we once grew to fruition'. Well no wonder my tiny shoulder is frozen. It's an exact replica of an ocean: full of penguins, rocky outcrops, algae, giant blue whales, French nuclear bombs, aircraft carriers, oil tankers and a couple of anchovies.

(Typically of the blinkered older generation who are not prepared to embrace new concepts, my mother claims I was born in a suburban hospital, and as far as she can recall there was not an awful lot of fruiting in an ocean going on at the time, but I think she's just trying to be Cleopatra: Queen of Denial.)

P.S. If you ever get cornered by one of these theory-spouting loons at a party, run like hell. Use both sides of your body.

Hippy Drippy

I've got a cold. 'Have you considered therapy?' asks a well-meaning hippy. No, I've considered vitamin C and a good lie down. If one more person suggests that because I'm sick I've got a bad attitude, I'm going to bite them.

This whole New Age crap seems to be extrapolated from the views of so-called gurus who think all disease comes from negative thoughts and emotions.

Unless we can get a grip on ourselves, there are going to be doctors saying, 'Well the good news is you've got leukaemia, but the bad news is you're really not thinking positively about your innermost experiences'. Already the New Age view seems to be that starving Africans are just not being perky enough about their life choices and double amputees, deep down, don't really want to travel.

It's hard enough dealing with some kind of illness without being told it's all your fault, you just have to 'heal your life' and 'the power is within you'. Positive thinking will help some people – the power of the mind can be inexplicable – but for others, it's just another way of saying 'it's all your fault, you slimy non-believing creepoid and you deserve to die, because you didn't believe us in the first place and if you're not getting better it's because you're just not doing it right like we tell you to'. Usually this stuff comes from people who deliver their suggestions in a low, 'caring' tone, as if to a small child.

Sure, stress is medically proven to whack out your immune system. It makes sense not to live your life on amphetamines, screaming at everybody, collecting automatic weaponry and embracing the theory of advanced self-loathing. Any doctor will tell you that. It makes sense to get second opinions and check out alternative therapies. And calm bubble baths and a positive attitude can't hurt. But they won't necessarily make you well again.

A masseur has asked me if I had I considered counselling for my menstrual disorder, a common disease called endometriosis. My explanation of combining herbal treatment with surgery as a last resort was not acceptable. Obviously there was some kind of mental and emotional problem. I was repressing my hidden reproductive urges. Clearly I was having some kind of emotional struggle with my ovaries. (Clearly I wouldn't be going back to her again.)

I went to a suburban Sydney GP with a recurrent stomach upset. She suggested I examine my conscience and read Louise Hay. I would rather have trashed her office. The medical problem, an allergy, was recognised by a herbalist after I told her my symptoms on the telephone, and cleared up within two days.

A much wackier herbalist, who turned out to be a Louise Hay devotee, told me of her weekend plans to go meet some aliens near Gosford. (It's a real conversation stopper, if you ever need one.)

Any admission of ill-health is now an invitation for amateur psychoanalysis. Tight shoulders? You're carrying too much of an emotional burden. Prostate cancer? You're not fond enough of your private parts, frankly. Sore throat? You're trying to say something that's kind of, you know, repressed. Breast cancer? Don't bother funding the research or looking at environmental factors, just fondle a crystal.

Maybe deep down sick people want to be sick. Maybe those damned plague victims in India are just metaphors for their own underdeveloped psyches. But maybe this whole thing's gone too far. Maybe somebody should explain to these people about germs, for a start. In a really 'caring' voice.

Hello?

A newish answering machine at our place startled everybody by speaking, after each message, in a computer-man kind of voice. 'Wednes. Day. 10. 37. A. M.', it would intone, with no regard for syntax. Eventually, I reckoned, we could progress to verbs, and then maybe, one day, the machine would say, 'Thursday. Six. P.M. My. God. I. Love. You'.

This answering machine proved a little more electronically surreal than that. If you didn't speak at all times, it would decide you were probably a fax machine. So, for example, if you were having a very intense conversation, and one party, say, just accused of being uncommunicative, had told the other party that this seemed a trifle overdramatic, and the first party had paused to draw breath before deciding whether to end the relationship once and for all or attempt a poignant reconciliation, then the answering machine would go PHWEEEARRRRRGHBBRRRRJJJ!!! and blow out everybody's ear drums, and refuse to believe you were not, personally, a fax machine, until it had sulked for a full 3 minutes and then it might give you a dialtone.

Spirituality and Other Dippiness

Or say you were on a business call and the person at the other end said, 'Steven Spielberg called. He wants to hear from you in the next 2 minutes and 59 seconds or that berzillion dollar deal will fall through. I'll just get the number – hang on it's in the pergola, could you hold on?' Pause. PHWEEEARRRRGHBBRRRRJJJ!!!

These electronic whimsies could be overcome by never allowing the conversation to flag and having a handy list of conversation points taped to the wall near the phone, including 'Is Barbara Cartland alive, technically speaking?', 'When Madonna gets mastitis and stretch marks after giving birth, will she release a coffee table book of the photos?' and 'Alexander Downer: toupee or not toupee?'. And you could hum to cover the silences caused by persons going out to the pergola.

This effect can be spoiled by the pergola person returning in a rudely stealthy manner and listening silently to your frankly tuneless humming and then frightening the bejeesus out of you by suddenly shouting, 'What is that FRIGHTFUL NOISE? Have we got a crossed LINE?'. After which there would be a shocked silence. (Immediately followed by PHWEEEARRRRGHBBRRRRJJJ!!!)

But, still, overall, bearable, kind of. But no longer. Because the answering machine has taken to – and, honestly, there has to be some kind of spookily demonic involvement – playing the messages *already received from other people* to the new caller. It is hard to overestimate the mortifying possibilities. Let me set the scene: Ginger de Owen Beeswax rings up. Instead of my outgoing message, she hears:

'**BEEP!** Hi, babe, it's your agent, Frangipani Noonar. You're completely broke and nobody wants to hire you. Probably best if nobody finds out. Hope you're well. Call me sometime next year. **BEEP!** It's your Mum. Got your message. Sorry to hear you're poorly dear, but I don't think it's genetic – at least, there doesn't seem to be a history of startlingly hairy bottom boils on MY side of the family. Try Vix Vapour Rub. **BEEP!** Hellair! It's Minx Whatmore. You're absolutely right – that new haircut of Ginger's does look like a welcome mat on the spin cycle! Ciao, darls!'

So a person of my acquaintance with Bachelor of Eng (Elect) after their name, a bootful of weeny tools and a brain that understands the difference between photons and the wires covered in red plastic looked at the problem long and hard, tickled the innards, read the instruction manual backwards, took a supplementary electronics refresher course and offered: 'Try unplugging it for a while and then plug it back in'. Oh, Phweeearrrrrghbbrrrrjjj.

Finding Your Inner Nanna

Welcome to the inaugural 'Getting in Touch with Your Inner Nanna' seminar.

Many of you are graduates of books like *Tentative Women Who'd Just Like to Kind of Stroll with the Wolves; Bonding with Your Inner Child;* and *Percussion in the Woods with Blokes Who Want to Be Blokey yet Sensitive, and Somehow Wildly Attractive, with a Legitimate Excuse to Cuddle Other Blokey People without Being Cuffed over the Noggin with a Wet Towel and Called a Woolly Woofter.*

Here at the Institut Space du Brain Prohibitifly Expensif, we aim to polish those therapy edges, and take you where no psychodrama has taken you before, in the mind-taxi of enlightenment. (See Olga if you need parking validation.) As a weekend retreat, it is important for you to know that you will not be leaving until Monday morning.

There is no way out. The perimeter is guarded by labradoodles and mother figures saying things like 'I'll be all right, dear. You go out and have a good time. I'll just stay here all alone and do the dishes'. If you do encounter any of the security staff, you should proceed immediately to the post-traumatic stress disorder wing, where Sven and Dave will Rolf you soundly for your trouble.

And now to the business at hand. I know that many of you here are proud graduates of the 'Where the Hell Is My Inner Child and Why Does It Always Want an Icy Pole' outward bound and executive bonding management skills dream analysis crystal aromatherapy course. Some of your colleagues are still in the recovery room as they have bonded with their inner child to such an extent that they now refuse to go to the toilet before long car trips, constantly inquire about whether we are there yet, and say there are spooky things under the bunks so they can stay up late. Matron reports steady progress, although stern measures have been taken in refusing Kinder Surprises to anyone who sings 'Kumbaya' during nap time and picks anyone else's nose.

Class 3a (i), Getting in Touch with the Inner, More Cranky You, should now be in D sector, as the volleyball courts are under water. Take your rubber bands, the small wads of chewed exercise book from your tote bag, and a nulla nulla from Stores. Please make sure your thermos has your name clearly marked; there have been incidents in the past.

Right. We here at the Institut are proud and excited about helping you to get in touch with your Inner Nanna. First, please turn to the person next to you, hug them, and repeat after me: 'You're not going to wear that outside the house are you?'. Good work. Lovely: we'll now break into small discussion groups. Group One: Knowing What to

Do with Cumquats or Chokoes. Group Two: When You Should Wear a Half Slip. Group Three: Sneaking Lollies to the Grandchildren even when the Parents Would Be Horrified. And Group Four: Advanced Martyrdom, with Particular Reference to Cooking the Whole Catastrophe on Christmas Day.

This afternoon, after bottling and reminiscence, we'll be taking an intensive workshop in linguistic Nanna phrasing, concentrating on 'Have you got a clean hanky?', 'You're just like your father' and 'Whoopsie, I accidentally poured all your tequila into the shrubbery'. Obviously, some of you will find that getting in touch with your Inner Nanna is a very emotional and confronting experience. Jeremy and Isotope will be moving among you informally with barley sugar, Tarzan jubes, crocheted throw-rugs and mince pies.

And don't forget our special offer this week, starting Tuesday: Getting in Touch with Your Inner Common Sense. $1235 for a two-day workshop in the Bahamas. Gather at the mini-bus on the south lawn at 7 a.m. sharp. BYO togs.

Fantasy Section

Due to a hideous pile-up at the cash register, I got stuck in front of the fantasy section of the bookshop the other day. This is not, as you might think, full of books called *My Night in a French Maid's Uniform* or *Girls in Red Thighboots* or *Mr Python Meets Someone Called Tracy*.

It is full of books called *The Faeries of Qantars*, *The Great Big Dragons of Zorg* and *The Enchanted Stone Thingie*. There are two main genres, roughly divided into: Dragons in Space and Medieval Trolls Run Amok in the Hinterland During Mysterious Medieval Type Times.

As the jostling at the cash register grew more rowdy, with vast numbers of the general public demanding not to buy the memoirs of former politicians, I had time to glance through a few. Unfortunately, Anne McCaffrey's *Dolphins of Pern* was snatched from my hands by a pushy maiden, but not before I had divined that the *Chronicles of Pern* was also available.

Pern is in outer space, where there are dolphins and dragons, and Torene comes to realise that her dragon could become the next Queen of the newly formed

Benden Weyr. Ms McCaffrey is author of twenty-one other books, including *Decision at Doona*. (Honestly.)

By contrast, Tad Williams' *Stone of Farewell* is not set in outer space, but is big enough to stun a dugong with, and part of a series of volumes that could safely dispatch approximately half-a-dozen dugongs. In a kind of Georgette-Heyer-romance-meets-The-Thunderbirds, Simon-the-former-kitchen-hand, now resident of the troll stronghold of Yiqanuc, uses his prophetic dreams to help trounce the evil Storm King, ruler of Osten Ard.

There are chambermaids, giants, dragons, your 'small, man-like subterranean creatures', monks, Ancient King John and a helpful twenty-one-page glossary in which we learn that 'Avi stetto' means 'I have a knife' and 'Ohe, vo stetto' means 'Yes, he has a knife'. Extrapolating, one sees that 'Ohe, ohe, ohe, vo dirty great stetto' means 'Do I have to tell you again, this bloke is completely fair dinkum about the knife'.

The Eye of the World, Volume 1 of the five-volume *Wheel of Time* by Robert Jordan, has back-cover praise from the increasingly well-known L. Sprague de Camp, who says it is a 'splendid epic of heroic fantasy'. The back-cover blurb reads like the sort of thing people say when they've been drinking Mezcal tequila: 'The Wheel of Time turns, and Ages come and go, leaving memories that become legend. Legends fade to myth, and even myth is long forgotten, when the Age that gave it birth returns again. In the Third Age, an Age of Prophecy, the World and Time themselves hang in the balance. What was, what will be, and what is, may yet fall under the Shadow'. ('And now, I shall eat the worm.')

The Eye of the World has some excellent stuff including wolves and a guy called Egwene.

The really good fantasy books, which run to about 10,000 pages, have a map. Maybe several. Raymond E. Feist's *A Darkness at Sethanon* has two maps because he's got a fair amount to fit in, including the Sea of Blood, the Confederation, Empires, the Great Sand Wastelands, the Endless Sea, the Straits of Darkness and also the Trollhome Mountains. Frankly, I don't think this sort of stuff will catch on.

As I adjusted my jerkin and prepared to take my leave, I warned the shop assistant. 'Dougalrod,' I said, 'mind the Marshes of Quarg.' 'And don't take any crook dolphins', he rejoindered menacingly, giving me the Sacred Sign of the Aardvole.

Ho, Ho, Ho Mary Christmas

Every few months a friend who hasn't been a news journalist for years still gets a fabulous press release from people claiming to have regular chats with the Virgin Mary. Well, one person, really, a chap called the Little Pebble. The Little Pebble always sends a photo of when he met the Pope at the Vatican, which was published in the *Nowra News* in 1985. (Try to keep up.)

Anyway, the Nowra mob keep their mailing-list recipients up to date on what the Virgin Mary has to say in her chats with the Little Pebble, and it is not very comforting, I don't mind telling you. I paraphrase from what they reckon Mary told the Little Pebble while she was in Wollongong.

The Little Pebble warns that a whole lot of repenting had better be nigh, because the present statistical breakdown shows that only 5 per cent of people go to heaven. According to the last missive, Mary has a special message in which she warns of the dangers of letting women onto sacred ground without headgear, and exhortations for women to wear opaque clothes (no trousers or short sleeves). Men are warned against shorts or tight clothing 'as these types of wear bring forward sin'. (I can't argue with Mary there. If I see a man in khaki-walk shorts, long socks and sandals I can barely contain my frenzied urges.)

Someone will try to kill the Pope and the forces of the Anti-Christ will march into the Vatican, the Pope will run away, Anti-Pope arrives, Third World War, a big miracle, atomic bombs, the full catastrophe followed by the Ball of Redemption. (Black tie only.) Eventually Jesus will triumph, all evil doers and the unrepentant will be severely deadibones and then just joy, peace and happiness for all the rest, although the world will end before the year 2000, which is just as well because according to this the mainstream Catholic Church is apparently run by flamboyantly attired New-Age Satanists. (Fancy!)

It does seem that any belief system – from Catholicism to New Age communism – has to suffer its very own bizarre offshoot mutations that leave mainstream religious organisations shaking their heads. Any rational, compassionate ideas can be put in the shade by the kookier bits. Particularly in North America. The idiosyncratic offshoot Nation of Islam, run by Minister Louis Farrakhan of Million Man March fame, for example, is dominated by his version of being given instructions aboard a UFO.

And let's not forget Joseph Jeffers from the Kingdom Temple and Yahweh's New Kingdom who ran away from the Baptists in America and in 1943 announced that he was, actually, come to think of it, Christ. He left his wife and took a young and pretty follower called Helen into

Spirituality and Other Dippiness

the desert to become the mother of his sacred child (did anybody spot the mid-life crisis?). Dr Jeffers decided Florida was the destination and even if it wasn't a desert a drought would turn it into one a bit later. (His wife got the car.)

Jeffers' more modern-day followers now stockpile weapons and occasionally are fired upon in sieges with the FBI.

While most of the 'kooks' seem harmless, one should never underestimate the need of some of the scarier evangelical outcasts for publicity, power and revenge. It seems that some people just aren't happy until those who don't accept their views come to a satisfyingly fiery end – the full Gymkhana of the Apocalypse. Hardly the true spirit of Christmas.

This year Christmas will be celebrated in many ways by many cultures: some grand, some humble. The original nativity scene is about to be performed by kindergarten kids as the three wise men with towels on their heads, bless their cotton socks (soon to be handpuppets). Whatever you believe, however you celebrate, season's greetings to y'all. See you at the Ball of Redemption (bring a plate).

Note: Extra facts from *Kooks – A Guide to the Outer Limits of Human Belief* by Donna Kossy, published by Feral House, Portland, USA.

Pope-ular Misconception

Women and the Pope – we're all in a frock, after all.

I don't know whether you noticed but the Pope and his mob came to visit the other day. The Press dusted down the adjectives used to describe an appearance of the Queen of England in the 1950s (radiant, gracious, fabulous frock) and went warpo about the man who looked like a well-dressed and benign acorn, at least viewed on my wee telly.

The Pope, it was reported, had something *extra*, something that set him above mere mortals. (As with the Queen, it's crucial to skirt the possible blasphemy. Cardinal Cassidy said, 'Of course, I wouldn't want anyone to think I was trying to put the Holy Father on an equal footing with Our Lord'.) A Mr Santamaria wrote that 'his appearance generates an electricity unmatched by anyone else on earth'. (It is to be imagined that Mr Santamaria has not ever attended The Big Day Out or Nelson Mandela.)

The Pope, media reports agreed, has a 'sharp wit'. The evidence for this included the fact that when he was served chicken Kiev, he said 'the chicken is from Kiev?'. Maybe you had to be there. According to the *Australian*

Spirituality and Other Dippiness 115

newspaper, the Pope was about to leave for India when he 'joked: "I will be eating curry and rice tomorrow"'. Is there something I'm missing here?

Much funnier was his exhortation that women who seek a true Christian concept of femininity should consider the role model of 'the free and active role assumed by Mary of Nazareth, the virgin mother of the Lord. In her, all women can discover the secret of living their femininity with dignity and achieving their own true advancement'.

So, girlies, there you have it: the one true way for all of us. Get married to a chippy, agree to be impregnated with the son of God by an angel disguised as a pigeon, and try explaining this new true dignity to your hubby over a cup of Horlicks one night. 'Darls, I have assumed the secret of true advancement in a free and active role. Incidentally, I'm up the duff. It's not yours: it's God's. He won't be paying maintenance. Did I mention it's garbage night?'

Now, the Pope is smart. He knows it's going to be an uphill battle convincing Catholics that women should be having virgin births, non-virgin births, any old birth in a storm for the term of their reproductive life. Young people have been deserting the church for decades, and many of its edicts seem to belong to other eras, when the church had less money and more influence.

So this idea of travelling the world making saints is an excellent one. We got Mary McKillop, and he got some great publicity. But it is not enough. There must be more work done if Catholicism and the monarchy are to survive in the robust millennium almost upon us.

It's time the Pope made saints of the Royal Family: let's have it official. There'll be no need for new photos: several pictures of Her Majesty in my collection feature icons worthy of a saintly panoply – tiaras, jewels, an incandescent light from within, a noble gaze into the distance, Phil, a sense of serene duty, gowns that flow like Golden Syrup.

Sure, there'll be some paperwork, but this is no time to be leery of red tape. Let's have St Elizabeth, Patron of Older Women with Vicious Corgis and Empty Handbags; St Diana, Patron Saint of the Shallow and Tragic; St Charles, Patron of Men Who Just Know They Might Be Useful if Only Someone Would Let Them; St Edward, Patron Saint of People Who Dislocate Their Jaws While Yawning, and of course the sentimental favourite, St Queen Mother, Patron of Drag Queens and Gin Drinkers. God knows, we've got to move with the times.

6
The Creativish Arts

Fair Enough Cobber Blue Beaut Mate

Why is it that foreign writers can't get Australians right? A recent episode of 'The Simpsons' had Australia's accent coming from the West End of London. (Clearly all the Australian actors in Los Angeles have been herded into 'Baywatch' waiting rooms.) Fictional Australians usually end up sounding something like a feral Chips Rafferty with a wildlife obsession.

In Jeanette Winterson's book *Written on the Body* an Australian demands of a door barger: 'Think you're on a kangaroo shoot or somethin'?'. (As rural readers will be aware there is an awful lot of barging through doors on a kangaroo shoot.) The character also says 'What are you staring at, digger?' and more inexplicably 'Don't play the Waltzing Matilda with me'.

In Paula Gosling's award-winning detective novel, *Death Penalties*, an Australian character refers to lies as 'dingo dribble' and remarks, 'The old wowser probably blew it all on beer' – a sentence nobody could write if they knew what a wowser is. In the same book a con-man plausibly poses as Australian by coming out with 'Aunty Dolly said you were a beaut sheila'; 'the bonzer thing to do'; and an attempted rape following 'you look real beaut'. As another of Gosling's characters might say, it's enough to give you the whim-whams.

Recently in London, some people thought it quite hilarious and polite to giggle, 'Oh, you're AUSTRALIAN. I hear none of the men wash and they don't know how to have sex'. I'm afraid I tended to reply, 'Actually Australian men are witty and charming and we all have fabulous sex that doesn't involve a Tory politician in suspenders and a piece of citrus fruit. In fact I'm going to have some more when I get home. (After we've discussed art and literature and cuisine and I've put all their flowers in huge vases.) With delicious Australian men. Heaps of 'em. In the transit lounge'. These English people would then do the grown-up equivalent of putting their fingers in their ears and shouting, 'La, la, la, la, la! Ha. Australian men: brutes all, and absolutely no manners'.

The general perception of Australian women is that instead of taking proper girly mincing steps, we stride around the outback in kangaroo-fur bikinis being called sheilas a lot. Perhaps it makes them feel better because deep in their hearts they know we have slightly more equal, much more sunny lives, with fresh food and beaches with sand instead of rocks – and they'd prefer to think we're all uncouth Queen-fondling sharkbait.

Where might our global trading partners get this image from? Is it just the exaggerated fiction that has cranky Russians saying 'Nyet!' and Nazis saying 'Schnell!' and

Americans saying 'Freeze!'? Do they extrapolate from grains of truth into mountains of stereotype? How is it that travel writer Paul Theroux comes to Australia and notices that we say 'prezzie' and 'cozzie' but claims in his book that Australians call Italians 'Spagettios' and we have also used the word 'Refujew'? (Come on, hands up – who's been teasing the travel writers?)

Then I wondered who the world has seen to give us this reputation. Barry McKenzie films? Rolf Harris? Peter Allen? Dame Edna Everage? Jason Donovan? Helen Reddy? Bryan Brown? Judy Davis? Jack Thompson? Rodney Marsh? Albert Namatjira? Germaine Greer? Margaret Court? Nah. The way Clive James leers at supermodels so horribly and comprehensively that his eyes disappear? Hmmm. 'Sylvania Waters', with that complete git who couldn't even make his own cup of tea, and Noelene with a voice like the desperate cries of traumatised rosellas? Double hmmm.

Anyway, do we care? Nup. Nothin' but a flaming bunch of pommy and septic galahs talkin' a load of dingo poop and gettin' their undies in a knot over some fair dinkum wombat-spanking, dead-set, true-blue . . . I do beg your pardon. I appear to be nodding off.

To Whom It May Concern

If a dedication at the front of a book tells us something of the author's attitude to relationships, we should not be disappointed at Hunter S. Thompson's in his solid gone gonzo book *Better than Sex: Confessions of a Political Junkie Trapped like a Rat in Mr Bill's Neighborhood*. 'To Nicole,' it reads, 'my vampire in the garden of agony.' (Keep taking the battery acid, Hunt.)

Before the concept of angel dust as a chemical came Robert Louis Stevenson's *Treasure Island*, devoted 'To Lloyd Osbourne, an American Gentleman, in Accordance with Whose Classic Taste the Following Narrative Has Been Designed, It Is Now, in Return for Numerous Delightful Hours, and with the Kindest Wishes, Dedicated by His Affectionate Friend, the Author'.

Rather formal, factual, boy-bonding acknowledgements seem to be a special forte of the English, leaving the more extravagantly adoring dedications to American books. At the start of *Elephant Bill* (1950), for example, Lieutenant Colonel J.H. Williams OBE rather gruffly writes, 'A Goodbye to the Elephants and Their Riders and to the Up-country Staff of Timber Assistants in Burma. Also as an appreciation of two Sappers, Bill Hasted and Tich Steedman, of the X1V Army, who did everything possible to help the Elephants in War'. Well, quite.

American comedian Rita Rudner's *Naked Beneath My Clothes* gets around the gush problem by valiantly admitting, 'I was going to thank some people but I was afraid I would leave someone out. Then I thought, I'll thank everyone, but I was afraid I would thank some people who didn't deserve to be thanked. So I decided not to thank anyone because the people who I was going to thank know who they are. Thank you'.

In *Bloom County Babylon: Five Years of Basic Naughtiness*, by American cartoonist Berkley Breathed, a delicious clue to his private life. 'To Sophie. My love, my life, my dog.' Other cartoonists go further. Lynda Barry's book *The Fun House* is in part dedicated to Matt Groening, 'Funk Lord of USA'. Groening, creator of 'The Simpsons', returns the compliment. In his *Work Is Hell*, the fine print reveals: 'Lynda Barry is Funk Queen West of the Rockies'. The acknowledgements of *Life Is Hell* go further, asserting boldly that Lynda Barry is Funk Queen of the Galaxy, but only after admitting that 'despite its title, this book is for Deborah'.

As all book editors know, 'For patiently standing by me and providing quiet, dinner and clean shirts all these years, to Beryl' suddenly might become, as the book goes to press, 'Dedicated to the youth and passion of Cyndii who understands while all around are deceiving HARRIDANS who run off with their aquarobics instructress at the most creatively crucial moments of one's LIFE'. Oldies and offspring are a safer bet, being less likely to change.

Susan Faludi's book *Backlash* is for her mother; Naomi Wolf's *The Beauty Myth* is for both parents. David Kirk, author of *Miss Spider's Tea Party*, dedicates it to his daughter: 'My darling Violet who is always kind to bugs'. Mr Kirk, says the book blurb, 'is considered by many to be central New York's finest bug poet'. (It is the word 'central' that makes that sentence so completely satisfying, I think.)

The author of *No Privacy for Writing: Shipboard Diaries 1852 to 1879*, Andrew Haffam, reports: 'It is customary to thank one's partner for his or her indulgence and understanding, which seems to me to be thanking her or him, in short, for being one's partner. By the same token . . . one might easily thank one's goldfish for being one's goldfish . . . Thank you Clare for being more than just a goldfish'. (Lucky old Clare, eh?)

Perhaps this is only rivalled by the last dediction in Zsa Zsa Gabor's autobiography: 'And to my husband Frederick – only we know how we feel about each other'. Thanks for nothing, Zsa Zsa.

Lost in the Translation

Madonna's recent interview with a Hungarian journalist was retranslated into English for the phrase 'I am not a test-mouse' to enter the language, and for cartoonist Garry Trudeau to write a spoof 'translation' in *Time* magazine, which, while much funnier than the original, many took for the real thing. So it's time that the idea of something being 'lost in translation' was joined by the concept of 'augmentation by translation'.

Take the eye-witness Paris catwalk fashion report in a Turkish tourist newspaper brought back from a recent holiday. In Turkish I'm sure it was pretty straightforward. But in English, it took on something special. '(Turks and their foreign friends) remember the bosphorus promises are exchanged overtley among them for a taste, of rakibay the bosphorus at the soonest time possible. At the same time a lean, and good-looking brunette Turkish model sways in a pastel coloured leather skirt on the podium . . . Turkish designers have an important say in the mens clothing as well and at that moment the smile of a Turkish male model clad in a black leather jacket meets the enthusiasm of the young french lady sitting amongst the guests. The blue of the meditterranean exuberantly rises.' (I'll bet it does, sailor.)

The fashion report goes on to say that 'fashion is the shine of this greeting and this old sphere we call our houses millions of people entraled by this shining'. And who among us doesn't need a damned good enthraling? Another article in the newspaper urged, 'If you're looking for handmade products antiquary, fresh vegetables and warm relationship go to Urla on friday an see the Malgaca bazaar which has 200 years'. This produced approximately the same level of puzzlement as the assurance on the side of the packaging on a Chinese coffee grinder bought in Preston: 'Flavour retailing shape of ellipse'.

So far I have had books translated from Australian into English (for England), American (for North America) and German (for Germany). Generally, the Americans change spanner to wrench, Uluru to the Grand Canyon (!) and ask if there is anybody likely to sue. The English tend to panic about finding a biscuit to replace the exact meaning and cultural resonance of 'Tim Tam', and the rest is surprisingly global, even phrases like 'in the nuddy' and 'flat out like a lizard drinking'.

The German was the most fun, with a very efficient and jolly novel translator sending queries like: 'Is "the wheat belt" an erotic reference?', 'Who or what is a Pollywaffle?' and 'What is a Besser brick and why is it up somebody's bum on page 167?'. (I had been trying to indicate a stiff posture in a metaphorical, obviously rather deeply *poetic* way.) It was somehow not surprising to note that the

Germans decided not to translate 'no worries' and left it in untouched.

I have tried to do the Madonna thing and translate it back again, a laborious project given that I don't speak any German. But I can only admire a culture that has words as long as *Lustcutters* (floating gin-palace, according to my cross-referencing), *wunschelrutenform* ('bendy') and *Zeitschriftenabonnements* (no idea). And what could I have written that came out as *'dem das Thermometer im Mundwinkel schlackerte wie Groucho Marx die Zigarre'*? Oh yes: but it sounds so much better than 'wiggling his pen like you-know-who's cigar'.

We already know that cosmetic companies call their creams 'Buste Galbeor Creme du Serum Thangie' because the French somehow seems more sophisticated than calling it 'Big Norks Ointment'. Even without the translation, things used to seem so much more romantic in the vairy attractif Frainch accent. 'Bonjour ma cherie' (g'day darls) had a special cachet (thingie) right up until the usual standard domestic program of inquiry (big fat bomb tests in the Pacific). Ciao.

Is That a Chicken in Your Pocket or Are You a Conceptual Artist?

Recent reports of a Satanic art exhibition in Balmain (Balmain?!) have me very concerned. The report said chicken heads had been nailed to the walls, dead animals were found on 'altars' and 'what appeared to be Satanic messages were scrawled on the walls, including "Bleed, little heart, bleed" and "The Church of the Everlasting Bitterness"'.

It doesn't sound like Satanism to me, frankly, although you can't be too careful these days. It sounds more like the inevitable result of an unhappy affair between a poultry farmer and a mad vegan artist. (Hell hath no fury like a woman scorned with access to a Buff Orpington.) 'Bleed, little heart, bleed' sounds like it could be a romantic lament, and 'The Church of the Everlasting Bitterness' could be the new Boy George single.

It puts me in mind of a police report I saw once on telly in Canberra. A sergeant, filmed at a desk, was appealing for help in a goat-torturing case. A school-type ruler had been dropped near the scene. 'The ruler appears to be inscribed with the words "Iron Maiden"', the sergeant said solemnly. 'Would anybody knowing the meaning of these words please contact the Manuka police station immediately.' The sergeant should get out more.

What appears to be of more interest was the reported fact that 200 people attended the opening of the 'Satanic' exhibition. What a shame they couldn't have had a camera out the front, like they do for movie ads, asking what people thought. 'I loved it, I want to see it again.' 'Yeah, great. I laughed, I cried.' 'Not as good as *Beverly Hills Cop 3*.'

It seems there has always been a rather magical bond between artists and livestock. Was the exhibition so different from all those years ago when artist Ivan Durrant dumped a dead cow on the steps of the National Gallery of Victoria, or from this year's Turner Prize-winner in England, you know, whatzizname who exhibited a pickled cow in a big fish tank? Well, why wouldn't they? It always makes the papers.

I'm thinking of nailing some snags and half a flathead to a plank in the City Square and writing 'Hail naughty Beelzebub, hey now, my boyfriend's back and your gonna be in trouble, hey now, hey now'. Should be good for a few column centimetres.

But perhaps the real question is, 'What is the artist trying to say, and do we give a toss?'. Could the message be, 'I am tougher than a number 15 boiling fowl past its use-by date'? Or might it simply be 'the postmodern use of the roofing nail tin for use in the narrative possibilities of nailing chook bits to the wall' or even 'If only I'd gone to life drawing classes I wouldn't be standing here in a rubber pinny with an Arts Council grant application and a blunt axe'?

Take Jeff Koons, the marketing artistic genius. Please. Give the man some space. His gigantic floral puppy in front of the Museum of Modern Art on beautiful downtown Sydney Harbour was desecrated by some art-hating fiend who secreted a dope plant among the blooms. (Police are looking for a Rastafarian called Lazlo.) Clearly the artistic solemnity of the artwork on a holistic level had been insultingly breached. If you people can't give the proper solemn respect to a giant floral dog, there's not much hope for you.

(Of course, if the chook bits mob turn out to be Satanists I shall say I told you so. I've got an artistic licence although the photo on it looks nothing like me.)

Jane Where Are Your Nipples: Video Reviews

Morning diary entry: Confined to a horizontal position with some kind of viral pestilence, and down to my last video, *Scott of the Antarctic*.

The last hairy Englishman dropped another frozen finger in the snow, muttering, 'It's all right sir, only a bit awkward, that's all. I'm quite well. Just a spot of indigestion after scoffing that last husky, I feel sure'. (Fall down in snow, severely dead.) 'Bad show', Scott said. 'Teddible.'

Afternoon: In a haze of viral insanity, I accidentally hire three exercise videos.

In the *Lean Routine* (1990), Jane Fonda plays a 53-year-old woman presenting an exercise video who may or may not have had two ribs removed to make her waist look smaller. Her costume is a see-through black lace body stocking and pixie boots, or maybe the body stocking is lined with fabric the exact colour of Jane's skin. It is very hard to keep one's mind on the hamstring lunge when you're wondering if Jane has any nipples to speak of.

Jane does the warm up and the cool down, and in between two instructors lead Jane and many other gristly

Americans through a series of exercise steps. The dialogue is not bad, perhaps the social realism slightly tainted by the number of times the dancers say 'Woo!' 'Uh-huh!' and laugh kind of wildly for no reason at all, unless it's Jane's cozzie.

I only needed to raise my left eyebrow to earn high praise from the instructor who looks a lot like Malibu Barbie, only she couldn't have been because my brother flushed her down the toilet when I was seven. 'Good!', she enthused. 'You're doin' great!' Jane took over and said to me, 'Talk to me! Say "Jane, I do you every morning!"' 'Jane,' I reply, 'where are your nipples?'. I am growing weaker.

Cher Fitness is introduced with a few disclaimers, including, 'The idea of this tape is not to kill yourself or beat yourself up'. Excellent plan. The chief points of interest of this video are Cher's outfits, and Cher's trainer Keli. Keli, an Australian I feel sure, makes Cher and some other Amazons do a lot of stepping up and down and not going anywhere. Luckily, Cher is wearing a bondage corset with tulle insets and I am able to occupy my fevered and failing faculties by adjusting my pillows and trying to read her tattoos.

This Tinkerbell of the amphetamine set then changes to singlet, braces, witch's britches and fishnet tights for the abdominal and back exercises, and a tightfitting cut-out number for 'hips, buns and thighs'. Cher admits only to nose and breast surgery, but if she exercises like this for hours every day, hopefully she will get to keep her own ribs. I don't know that I'll live to see it. The light is failing.

Raquel Welch's *Body and Mind* is based on the work of a very well-respected stress and yoga expert, whose work cries out to be translated through the presentation of the celebrity who brought us films such as *One Million Years BC; Fuzz; Mother, Jugs and Speed* and *Lose 10 Pounds in Three Weeks*. Raquel explains how she used to be so stressed that once her hand was shaking too much for her to hold the eyebrow pencil.

Raquel's teeth are the colour of Liquid Paper, and she looks at least thirty years younger than she really is, which must be because she is not stressed any more, her eyebrows are on straight and she wears thongs. 'Trust in God', she advises.

That's easy for her to say. It seems a pity, but I cannot write more. You will know from this account how bravely I faced my fate. Farewell. Please look after my begonias and help yourself to the last chocolate bisc . . .

A Shameful Addiction to Wicker

Circulation is reported to be rising for *Vogue Living*, *Belle*, *Home Beautiful* and *Better Homes and Gardens* magazines. Well, at least it isn't just me. Other people are also tragically hooked on this antidote to contentment, this land of covetousness – this Deco Porn.

I first realised that I had a problem with interior decoration pornography when I started buying the magazines even though I don't have a house, or a garden, to speak of. Certainly not one that belongs to me and that I could do any decorating in without risking my bond, no matter how much that mission-brown Laminex in the kitchen makes me want to cry.

All those photos of gorgeous fabrics – silken, slippery, sensuous, sliding over curtain rails and caressing embroidered Irish bed linen whispering . . . ahem . . . excuse me. I just like to watch.

Polished floors the colour of honey and just as shiny, and corrugated-iron designer beach shacks with seventeen bedrooms opening to the sea at 48,000 separate windows. Unsmudged kitchens; bathrooms with see-through soap, all new and unscummy; mirrors without toothpaste splatters. I want that life in the pictures. Except for the clean, solemn children that match the wallpaper (I wonder which came first). And all the houses are neat, and there is storage space for everything and no undies on any of the lampshades.

Just as Food Porn photographers cheat by lacquering fruit and substituting mashed potato for the sorbet, one suspects that the house stylists cheat by moving the furniture, shooting with wide-angle lenses and bringing in pot plants, flowers and cushions for the day. It is not absolutely clear who supplies the children.

In Deco Porn World there are antique Sicilian paving tiles, vast lily ponds, idle chatter about the romance of wicker, split system air conditioning and the 'harmonious juxtapositioning of nature and functional form' (which I think is code for rainforest timber). The houses have names like Flouncimere and Cashmount, and as a rule they were built for a sea captain late last century.

The most exotic aspect is all the photographs of apartments and houses owned by 'young professionals' — all decorated in pristine white. You wouldn't want your polar bear to go missing. Floors, walls, ceilings, tables, chairs, beds, in fact everything except whitegoods are white. (The whitegoods are shiny stainless steel.) This is known as minimalism, the new simplicity or the White Furniture Policy. It is difficult to say whether you would need to reupholster a pure white couch hourly, or just weekly. Perhaps you're just not supposed to go anywhere near it.

In Deco Porn World there is a woman in an ad so utterly THRILLED about the concept of parquetry she has to just hurl her legs in the air even though she's wearing a skirt. This ad is supposed to make you buy parquetry, unless it's trousers.

The magazines also have lots of hints, from how to spruce up a lampshade with just some rick-rack and $3000, to some elementary pet psychiatry. ('If you leave your dog at home all day it will probably eat the white couch.')

In Deco Porn World even the old furniture is expensive. Remember the distressed furniture look of the 1980s? Well it's thoroughly traumatised by now. Coolgardie safes and old bits of wood with makeshift flyscreen panels go for hundreds, if not thousands of dollars.

'Why,' asks *Vogue Apartments*, 'do so many modern urban groovers dress in grunge and decorate their homes with salvage? . . . supporters believe that these items (although manufactured in the past) will become historic representations of 90s style as surely as Alessi kettles represented the 80s . . .'

Or, might I humbly suggest, people buy secondhand stuff because they reckon $475 is a bit steep for a kettle.

What's My Line?

It all started with *Life's Little Instruction Book*, by H. Jackson Brown, Jnr, a tiny book with a single homily, or just a couple of sentences of advice on each page. Nine million copies later, Jackson Jnr is up to Volume 3 and down to 'Improve even the best sausage biscuit by spreading on a little grape jelly' appearing two whole suggestions before 'Respect your elders'.

At least since the Bible's Proverbs, and through the *Little Red Book of Mao Zedong Thoughts* (including 'Revolution Is Not a Dinner Party' but presumably not 'Get Me Another One of Those Teenagers in Pigtails'), pithy 'thoughts' have been best-sellers. Now they're everywhere and nobody could be more thrilled than writers. One sentence, or one paragraph per page, tops! Or a few sentences appearing on the same page bearing no relation to each other!

Even when paragraphs lead on from one another, brevity can be made virtuous. Especially in *Become Happy in Eight Minutes*, written by 'advertising ace Siimon Reynolds' (the sort of title and author that renders satire redundant). Every second page of the book is entirely taken up by a quote on happiness by somebody who isn't Siimon. Siimon's parts are printed on each right-hand page, and in a kindly gesture to the sight-impaired they are printed in quite large type.

Other Australians have cottoned onto the brilliant desk-calendar-thought-for-the-day-as-book idea. John Laws first came out with his *Book of Irreverent Logic*, which is often one sentence per page with the first letter of the sentence presented very elaborately in ye olde worlde scrolly style, to indicate ye anciente wisdome. One of the wisdoms is, 'Smile if you are not wearing panties' (formerly, as far as this reader can recall, a 1970s American bumper sticker).

Mr Laws' latest, with up to a whole paragraph on a page, *John Laws' Book of Uncommon Sense*, includes 'You will find that violence and decency rarely go hand in hand'. (Go on with you.) And 'Tyranny will only survive as long as freedom is abused'. (Get right out.)

Departing briefly from type, Bryce Courtenay's offering, *A Recipe for Dreaming*, is printed on lovely paper and beautifully illustrated. It builds to a crescendo of one-liners on one-pagers, notably 'When we chop down the tall poppies only the weeds remain' and 'Why do all folk songs sound the same?'. (Bryce, the answer, my friend, is blowin' in the wind.)

Outback Wisdom — Sara Henderson Looks at Life is pretty much in the same vein with 'Ability has no gender' and 'Judge people by the colour of their soul . . . not their skin'. (Although her exhortation to 'Approach all creatures on equal terms' is a somewhat alarming philosophy for a beef exporter.)

The author of *Meditations for Women Who Do Too Much* has followed up with *Native Wisdom for White Minds: Daily Reflections Inspired by the Native Peoples of the World*. The author observes of Aboriginal spiritual life, 'For some Westerners, this has resulted in a drive to know and understand Aboriginal "secrets"'. (Not to mention bulldoze their sacred sites.)

Some poor editor has made an attempt to Australianise *1001 Ways to Be Romantic* with 'David Jones, Grace Bros. and Myer all have great end-of-season sales' but other helpful items remain, such as the price of a Concorde ticket and the US telephone number for sending chocolate chip cookies.

I've started to compile a list of my own thoughts that include 'Have I left the iron on?', 'If you don't want to cook maybe you could get takeaway', 'If I am judged by the colour of my soul, what if it is beige?' and 'I think my foot's gone to sleep', so I'm already halfway to a publishing contract. And as my friend Cheerful Davo always says, 'Tread softly but carry a large beef jerky'.

7
Oeuvre-indulgence

Nuevo Foodo

Some of you may have noticed the upsurge in reference to New Food. Like the reported sightings of the New Man, this has caused some confusion, and lots of people thinking, 'Surely this isn't what I ordered!'. Allow us to assist you, with our Handy Form Guide to New Food. You never have to be alarmed by a lunch menu again.

Brioche
A suburb of Tuscany, a French region where food was invented. The capital is Bocuse. (Watch out for my new book, *Where the Hell Is Tuscany, Anyway?*)

Coulis
Anything squished for long enough is a coulis. It is always underneath something.

Compote
Something that has not been squished quite long enough to be a coulis.

Braise
To frighten. As in, 'Take that bloody duck down the back paddock and give it a good braising!'.

Bavarois
Posher flummery arrangement.

Blancmange
Pronounced 'WOOSTER-SHEER'.

Junket
Overseas restaurant review.

Arugula!
The sound of a rude car horn.

Fetta!
A sudden cry of great surprise.

Bisque
A hat of the toque family, worn by many Belgian chefs.

Fried Egg
No change from old measurements.

Fried Brie
Oh, lordy.

Salsa
Sexy Latin music. From the Spanish, 'To flirt with the biggest onion in the room'.

Turmeric
A dull party lettuce, with a bland, tedious taste, from the English, 'Turgid Eric'.

Bed
As in, 'served on a bed of parsnip snides'. Avoids the use of the phrase 'a runny pile of'.

Al Fresco
The man who invented Cheese In A Can.

Dill
As above.

Fool
Let's not go on about it.

Rutabaga
Capital of Zaire, home of the yam coulis.

Marinated
Legless. As in, 'If you're marinated and drive, you're a bloody idiot'.

Creme Anglais
Cream of England.

Creme Brulee
Cream of Brule.

Bulghur Wheat
Wheat that is quite often disquieting in its frankness.

Antipasto
Reformed pasta abuser.

Mkate Wa Ufute
Zanzibarian pancakes.*

Okra
A talk-show host's recipe book. As in, 'I didn't even have to write this okra myself and it's making me a fortune. I'm going to try an exercise video next!'.

Naan
Person with the best old-fashioned mince pie recipe.

---

*A recipe for Zanzibarian pancakes is in the ambitiously titled *The World in Your Kitchen, Vegetarian Recipes from Africa, Asia and Latin America*, by Troth Wells, published by Virago Press, which is, of course, a robust instrument for crushing nuts (archaic).

Tuile
The noise a mouse makes when you stand on it (colloq.). Also, a ballerina frock fabric.

Lentils
The only known food that in itself causes flatulence but as a spoken word cures insomnia.

Daal
Traditional end to a drink order in many homes, almost archaic in some regions. Example: 'Get us another beer, daal'.

Steaming Hot Chaat
What would follow such a request in some regions.

Osso Bucco
The name given to any Eastern European whose military decorations have dangled in the soup.

Guacamole
To be entirely sane. As in, 'Leave him alone, sister. He ain't the whole guacamole'.

Witlof
A new lettuce, so-named for its close relative, a Star Trek character. In the tradition of a dessert full of fat and sugar being named after a tall, thin, highly-strung person called Pavlova.

Tapas
Beer and olives.

McMuffin
No listing.

Baby Spinach
Now out of fashion. Replaced by Spinach Puberty Surprise.

Polenta and Gorgonzola
Two martyred saints who were put to death in 325 AD by St Ethelred the Disgruntled, who just wanted some cheese on toast.

Curly Endive
Amusing carrot shavings.

A striking whim of Pert Aubergine Paupiette, tinkling on a futon of hairy-fluted pilaf, embracing a marinated frock of liaised gravlax with fritter au glazed goat gusset, followed by a distressed Mango Idiot for dessert
Order the chook.

White Christmas Dreaming

Did you ever do Home Ec at school? I did, because girls weren't allowed to do metal work, which was on at the same time. (This, I believe, is what has turned me into the rabid foaming feminist man-eating nympho tragic envier of welders everywhere that I am today.) What I can remember of Home Ec was a cooking teacher who made her mouth look like a cat's bum when I showed her my White Christmas.

White Christmas, for those of you who don't know, is a sweet, hardened slice of confectionery, somewhat like nougat would be like if it was left in the desert for as long as it takes nuclear waste to stop being radioactive. Let's be fair. If the building sector ever got their hands on my White Christmas the entire concrete slab industry would be on the ropes.

Like the square of the hypotenuse and a modern dance called the logarithm, I have found no use for White Christmas in grown-up life. I wish I could remember my times tables, instead of knowing the capital of Albania. (San Paolo.) Frankly school was all downhill after Clag-wrangling in kinder, as far as I'm concerned.

What would really have been useful in Home Ec was how to spot a real-tasting tomato, shopping without tears, and what to make for tea when there's only Tim Tams, a turnip and two packets of agar agar in the fridge. The only other thing I remember cooking in Home Ec was a cake, although it may have been a beret made out of flour, now that I reflect.

Something of my distaste for Home Ec was that the actual cooking, from memory, took place in the same room as the rat dissections. (Perhaps it was just the same building, or maybe they wiped the benches with industrial strength ammonia afterwards.)

Listen, I said, when the subject of rat dissection came up. I could not be more disinterested in the bits of a rat nature has seen fit to shield us from by way of inventing the outside of a rat. If you really think I would be edified by the view, I am quite prepared to look at a black and white diagram. As far as I'm concerned it is only necessary for one person, ever, in the entire world, to cut up one rat. Then they can travel widely, telling vast throngs of the interested public what it looks like, with the aid of an overhead projector, a pull-down map of Albania and a plastic model with moving parts.

This view was not acceptable and on the day everyone had to cut up a rat each (don't jostle, children, there's one each and more for afters), I went for a bit of a stroll. I got a detention, but worse than that, was turned off science for life.

I have been deprived of the romance of photons and am still frightened my atoms might drown in the bath. And I've only recently been able to wear navy blue again. (Ask a woman what colour she doesn't like wearing and ten to one it was her school-uniform colour.) And as for White Christmas, I recommend it to you all. Here is the recipe from memory, as made by Year 9 nutrition elective.

White Christmas
Combine in a large beaker the following: 27 pounds of white sugar. (Reserve one pound of sugar.) Eight gills liquefied lollies. Five cans condensed milk. Three sultanas. Tbspn Copha. Tspn squishy red glacé cherry things. Spakfilla to taste. Heat over Bunsen burner in a double-sided melon pan until maths. Sprinkle with cinnamon and rest of white sugar. Serves: one. Calories: nine billion. Serve while still hot. Allow to cool. Find the tooth and take it with you in a cup of water to the nearest emergency dental clinic.

Ho, Ho, Berloody Ho

No, it's not just you. We're all thoroughly sick of ho, ho, berloody ho, and would rather stick harpsichords up our nostrils than deal with Christmas more than one second longer than necessary.

Many of you will be seeking help for Post-traumatic Toys 'R' Naturally Not Supplied With Batt'ries Stress Syndrome and up to your ears at this point in wrapping paper and Mighty Morphin Power Rangin' All-speaking, All-weeing Pretty Pony Baby Lego Over-exciters with tantrum function and bonus two-volume Sleighed Alive CD. It has slipped the mind of others that they look like a dork in a paper hat, and Aunty Eileen's been on the cooking sherry since the eighth day of Christmas. (It is about this time that you should mail your credit card to Alan Bond, safe in the knowledge that things couldn't get worse.)

It is, according to unconfirmed reports, the season of goodwill. I would have been prepared to go along with this until the Stain On The Couch Incident. It's not that I'm particularly fond of the couch, although a certain amount of bonding is to be expected, given that it took four months to arrive after I paid for it in cash at one of those shops that whack a sprauncey colour catalogue in your cakehole every few months.

(Green? they said. Green. That's a bit of an ask. 'It's in your colour cattle dog', I said: 'Look, here's the picture. Couch. Green. Big, Green Couch'. 'Ah, two-seater in Forest Canopy Surprise', they said. Three weeks, tops. Ho, ho, berloody ho.) Anyway, I had arranged myself languidly on the 'Surprise' last week, having a late supper of taramasalata, bread and butter, sticky cheese, raspberry cordial and sump oil, when the news came on.

(By way of warning, you hear a lot about how television can cause violence, not to mention low-level sexual references.) On to the screen oozed 'failed entrepreneur' Christopher Skase and his wife who is called, I'm very much afraid, Pixie. Australian authorities have been trying to recover Señor Skase by sea mail from somewhere in Spain, where he is believed to be living so high on the hog that the big porker is tiring of the caper and in need of a good lie down. (If that's a failed entrepreneur, how do the successful ones live?)

The newsreader said that Señor Skase has been released from a Spanish pokey and would not be required to return to Australia, which is just as well as one can imagine what it would be like if he ever got to court, at approximately $58,600 per QC for each 'Buggered if I can remember'.

So I gingerly placed supper on my knees, adjusted my extended tibia for extra balance, and lifted my glass in salute to the legal system of Australia. The announcer said, and I can't stress this enough, 'Mr Skase has compared his ordeal to that of Nelson Mandela'.

Well YOU try getting taramasalata out of a cushion zipper and your ears simultaneously.

I have applied to the Australian Securities Commission for the extradition of Señor Christopher, on two counts. He is to be charged with causing Grievous Harm To The Concept Of Forest Canopy Surprise with utterly aggravating damages, and two zillion billion million trillion and eighty-four counts of Comparing Himself To Somebody Interesting And Courageous With The Light Of Justice Inside Him Who Could Fairly Be Described As Charisma On Legs.

Frankly, he's going down.

Which reminds me, as poet Johnno Donne once said, in the heat of passionate Yuletide revelation, no man is a berloody island. And to our knowledge, not many girlies resemble a rocky outcrop or promontory. So Merry Isthmus, and a Preposterous New Year to youse and yours. Mind you remain standing for the Queen's message, or at least some portion of the day.

Passive Parenting

Never mind about passive smoking – the lawyers are already onto it. What about passive parenting? There you are having a quiet cup of tea in a restaurant and somebody's toddler is halfway up your leg going the grope in your gado gado when you hear a tinkly voice from the other side of the room: 'Did I have a two-year-old with me when I came in? Oh, there you are Drago, darling, aren't you good: as quiet as a mouse'. Yeah, a 10 kilogram mouse with tantrum function.

A friend recently gently reminded a parent at a baggage carousel that considering their darling cherub continued to poke his fingers into the moving beltway the mother might like to know that a child doing the same thing in the same spot two weeks earlier had cut his finger very badly. 'Yeah, thanks', said the mother, sarcastically, turning her back on the still-poking child and our Cassandra.

At Sunday brunch in a Melbourne restaurant a man read the paper as his three-year-old tried everything to get his attention: starting with poking all the other customers, ending with emptying the sugar container across the table before adding his drink and bit of his father's newspaper

Oeuvre-indulgence

and a good shrieking, and poohing his corduroys rather comprehensively. Well, you can't blame him; by the time he was trying to set fire to three patrons, a tablecloth and the waiter's armpit hair, his father finally had to notice him.

Overseas recently I watched as two children relentlessly poked with sticks some caged birds as their parents, German tourists, laughed merrily and occasionally told them to stop. In a Sydney cafe, parents brought in small children on a sunny day, handed them a soccer ball and then told them they could NOT PLAY WITH IT INSIDE and they WEREN'T ALLOWED TO GO OUT ON THE ROAD. These parents clearly expected their six-year-olds to sit down, order a macchiato and discuss the Tarantino oeuvre with special relation to post-wankerism.

Like victims of passive smoking who eventually develop emphysema, victims of passive parenting end up haggard and wan, nervously eyeing children who wander close to the traffic, trying to have a business conversation while distracted by the action across the road as somebody else's nine-year-old is attempting to insert into a postbox slot a St Bernard with a 5 cent stamp on its bum (degree of difficulty 8.9).

Then there's passive conversation: the number of people who use mobile phones on public transport or in a pub or cafe is rising by about 679 million an hour. The other thing that is rising is the voices of people who use mobile phones. And what do they yell? Do they yell interesting facts, or lascivious gossip? No, they yell things like

'HOW'S VERA?'. The other fifty-six people forced to listen to this conversation do not usually wish to be kept apprised of Vera's relative in-the-pink-ness. In fact they are beginning to wish Vera ill.

And passive nerdiness is on the rise, too, as one might be forced to hear the following computerspeak, however unsolicited: 'Seventeen-and-a-half megs of joosh and a spraunced SCSI 56.3 booted power lulu 6100/66 mousiepants on megaport whoopsie sideways MAC IBM SIMM ROM RAM BIMM BAM A WOP BOP A LOO WAH A LOP BAM BOOM'. At which point the eyes become double-glazed.

There's only one way to deal with it all: get passive aggressive. Hand back unwanted toddlers with the line, 'Excuse me, I think you might have dropped this'; tell the mobile phoner there's better reception OUTSIDE, actually about three kilometres down the road especially if you stand on a 45 degree angle; and faint at the mere mention of megaports.

'Tis the Season to Drink Bolly

I have been asked to convey to you my thoughts about the more challenging portions of the holiday season (or what one festively seasoned pal refers to sternly as 'the pisstivities'). Social scientists would do well to study why at this time of the year everybody is either legless drunk, hungover, frantically hysterical and exhausted, cranky as all get out, clinically depressed or Father Christmas.

It is this very special time of year that I am reminded of a gaily colourful poster produced many years ago for the Women's Christian Temperance Union called, if I recall correctly, 'For a Happy Party, the Clever Hostess Serves Fruit Drinks'. For a happy party at this time of the year, the clever hostess would serve Valium and Eno and have a policy in place for the suppression of small arms fire near the barbecue. She might also consider being interstate at the time.

Because the period around Christmas and the New Year should be marked on the calendar as Barking Mad Drunks Week. They are everywhere. They lurch out of pubs and straight onto the road. They turn up at the door with a bottle of Bundy asking for someone called Barry. They insist on telling you about the time they were abducted by aliens in Cooma. They burst into tears on a bus and try to make the driver take them to the Big Pineapple (for sentimental reasons). They climb the Christmas tree at the office party and attempt to eat a Christmas tree bauble.

Then they sit down in the lift singing 'God Rest You Merry Whatsyerface, Let Nothing La La La! Rudolph With Yer Nose So Thingie; On The Feast Of ... Stephen From The Mail Room! Let's tongue kiss!'. Seasonal drunks will get very cross if you do not share their brilliant ideas for entertainment, such as 'Way-heyyyy! Lesh all drive down the median strip, shouting!' and 'There's only banana liqueur and Guinness stout left! Yippee! Cocktails!'. Any gentle attempts at dissuasion will be met by them stealing your trousers, calling you a party pooper or falling unconscious into the coleslaw. And that's just the teenagers.

It may be that my time spent living in the Northern Territory has prejudiced me against people who think a slab of Melbourne Bitter is morning tea. It may be that I have certain wowser tendencies. Which is not to say that I don't get drunk. I do so get drunk. It's just that during the time that I am actually drunk I imagine I am being terribly sophisticated and amusing. It's only afterwards that I remember I pulled my frock over my head and recited *The Man from Snowy River* to an empty room and then threw up in the host's letterbox. It is much easier to be horrified by other drunks. I find it very hard to be horrified at myself when I am drunk, because at that time my judgement is impaired by alcohol. (Logic has always been a strong point.)

There are three major phases of driving behaviour over the festering season. Firstly, the pre-Christmas free-for-all. In this preliminary phase it is up to any car in front of yours to park suddenly in the middle of the street, turn left from the right-hand lane, go 2 kilometres an hour on the freeway, or try to drive through a fast-food joint that doesn't have a drive-through facility.

This is closely followed by the Christmas to New Year weaving all over the road interlude, and culminates in the New Year's Eve maelstrom of driving on the wrong side of the road or the wrong way down a one-way street, or, ideally, rear-ending the booze bus and attempting to blow into the constable's left ear. This New Year's Eve phase may only be varied by waiting until 8.30 a.m. for a cab.

I'm off to be terribly sophisticated and amusing. Taxiiiiii!!!!

Grunge Gambling

Trawling through a first-hand bookshop recently, desperate for a copy of Miss Tabitha Minx's new grunge novella *Hurry Up, Trevor, for Christ's Sake*, or the grunge short stories classic, *F***ing Nothing Much* by Bruce Flange, I happened across a yellowing tome by Professor John Cohen called *Chance, Skill and Luck*, and was desperate for the distraction.

I know it's really groovy to read the New Wave of grunge fiction, but there is only so much unsatisfying sex, bad drugs and dead-end jobs I can take. (Even vicariously.) I know it's gritty reality, in some cases even well written, but it just makes me want to read about Enid Blyton's Famous Five. (Say what you like about Anne, but she probably didn't share a needle with George, pass the ginger beer spiked with Rohypnol to Dick or wait for Julian to stop having his way with Timmy in the caravan. What Uncle Quentin was doing in the tower with those suspicious foreigners doesn't bear thinking about. Probably idly tattooing them with an impact drill.)

Anyway, it was quite refreshing to be lured from the world of fashionably fluoro-lit pukey bits to Prof. Cohen's book, which introduced several amazing facts. One of these is that when you get a bunch of bus drivers shickered on whiskey in a 'controlled' experiment, they will overestimate their skill in driving through narrowly placed posts.

Presumably, if you give a bunch of bus drivers enough whiskey the drivers may be under the impression that it's a good idea to get on the bus roof in the nuddy and do the hokey cokey, but this was not included in the Professor's study. Basically, it seems to prove that people who get pissed think they are luckier. (Perhaps this accounts for the serving of alcohol in casinos? Surely not.)

Then I read elsewhere that punters had lost at least $1.3 billion in six months at the Melbourne casino last year. It can't all have gone down the back of the casino couch, so now I want to be a casino owner. I want to attract the hungry, the desperate, the frightened, the bored. I want to convince them that they have nothing to lose because they are nothing. I want a society that will keep producing poor, uneducated, unemployed, under-utilised people whose best chance at a privileged life is about sixty-seven trillion to one out there on my sticky-carpeted game floor.

Why yes, I'm going to have telly ads made with healthy women who show their tummy buttons and toss their long hair, ha ha, and men who look like they are in charge of things, G'day, how are ya, all milling around showing all their teeth when they laugh, punching the air and looking well fed with new clothes and eyeing each other off and knowing they'll get what they want later on, and as if they'd never have a wee under a roulette table. And in the ad they'll be talking and laughing with each other, not hunched silent and red-eyed and grinding their teeth with a hollow, numbed look in their eyes, like the real patrons. There'll be a waiting list for counselling gambling addicts. They'll lose their jobs and get legless on cheap port and be sarcastic to their partners about how much money they make and forget personal hygiene and just generally get completely fed up with a joyless grind characterised by morbid dread in which nobody ever even gets kissed properly, and it's a looped Loserville life of hideous poverty traps and grinding disadvantage that carves a caustic bitterness deep on the cortex. I will explain there is no way out of the grunge life, unless you like the usual odds.

And then they can all write a really groovy book about it.

The Peerless Fearless

The usual joke-shop fare of fake vomit and wax fingers (designed to create hilarious repulsion) and farty whoopee cushions and black-foaming toothpaste (designed to create hilarious embarrassment) is supplemented by something rather more curious: the rubber spider. The rubber spider is designed only to cause hilarious *fear*. (Or perhaps a humorous heart attack, caused by fear.)

Fear of spiders is common enough that almost everyone knows what arachnophobia means, even if they don't watch movies based on Stephen King novels. The logistical problem with the hilarity of a rubber spider is that one has to presume one's victim is arachnophobic, and these days there's no guarantee of that – arachnophobia has a lot of competition. (No point in dangling a hairy-legged doppelganger in front of somebody who says, 'Ah, from the genus *Isopoda immanis*, if I'm not mistaken'.)

The Cambridge Factfinder lists so many phobias it's fair boggling. Some are common: spermatophobia (fear of germs); cynophobia (dogs); hypegiaphobia (responsibility); kakorrphiaphobia (failure), and neophobia (fear of newness). And who doesn't have a milder version of the more psychotic or obsessive fear of death (thanatophobia); blushing (ereuthrophobia); or robbery (harbaxophobia)?

There are unarguably debilitating but much rarer ones: barophobia (fear of gravity), mastigophobia (flogging), and chrometophobia (fear of money). How many cases can there possibly have been of Auroraphobia (fear of the Northern Lights), for heaven's sake? It just goes to show that a mind can fixate on anything if the wrong wire is spliced near a neuron junction of the brain's chemical switches. And to show that one person's wall-scaling terror is another's dinky rubber tarantula.

There was no record of phobiaphobia – a possibility worthy of consideration since I saw an interview with the mother of the little seven-year-old 'pilot' who was killed in a plane crash while trying to break a record as the world's youngest pilot. The dead child's mother said that her children were not allowed to play with children's toys and were trained not to know fear.

Fear is not such a bad idea. It has had some good results since the first bison ran at the first caveperson and the caveperson scarpered up a tree. For example, are you afraid of what might happen if you stick a barbecuing fork in the closest power point? Yes? Good. If a man in a balaclava comes into your room in the middle of the night, would you a) offer him a Campari and a crumpet with lemon butter on it, or b) run shrieking to the neighbours? Would you poke a panther with a stick? Throw a custard pie at Peter Costello? (That doesn't count.)

Of course, one of the gorgeous things about little kids is their fearlessness, their endearing habit of speaking without knowing much about their subject, and their cute, wide-eyed innocence. But in a grown-up the same qualities usually denote what we know as a 'complete bimbo'. A person totally without fear is either ignorant or fully unconscious.

Real bravery can only exist within fear. Those who take on the Nigerian Government, a corrupt local cop, or the office bully are courageous because they are frightened and they act despite their fear. You can *like* them both, but who would you rather have on your side, Nelson Mandela or Dopey the seventh dwarf? Sure, you say, but Dopey had an easier life. Well let me remind you that Dopey worked in an underground mine before labour laws and had to sleep in one room with six other guys who couldn't cook or clean and didn't have access to cable sports television, only one of whom was Happy. Scary.

8
Women's Rites

Berloody Feminists

I was trying to read a review of a book about the Second World War when the first paragraph exploded. 'There was a time when Australian men valued virtues such as courage, mateship, stoicism and dependability in times of crisis ... these days, feminists have sullied those male virtues with ridicule and made them vices ... [a time] when men could still love and sustain each other without feminist scorn.'

Berloody feminists. Not content with frightening the horsies and causing the Bosnian situation *and* the decline of literacy, have they been out sullying the diggers?

It will certainly come as a surprise to many of the nurses, sweethearts, wives, and mothers, war workers all, who recognised courage, mateship, stoicism and dependability because they displayed those virtues themselves and relied on them in the menfolk they loved and missed.

Many women wanted to stay in the workforce after the war, believed it was terrible that girls caught in the passion of those minute-by-minute times died from backyard abortions, and deplored the double standards of the day that meant single mothers found it so terribly hard to get by. In other words, many had 'feminist' ideals. Fancy.

I wasn't there then, but I, too, admire the virtues of the soldiers. I wish they didn't have to go to war, but I do honour them for their bravery and thank them for their sacrificing their best intentions and their boisterous, invaluable young minds and bodies. I'm glad they loved and sustained each other. I'm in awe of the disorganised hell they were sent to and brought back in their heads. I've not heard them ridiculed by a feminist, or by anybody else, but perhaps I don't get out enough.

I did read an interview with a writer once, photographed in lipstick and a short skirt. She said 'feminists' had 'told' her not to wear such things. I have heard of girlies who still say that frocks and lipstick are treacherous to the women's cause, much as I hear about the Tasmanian Tiger. I have never come across one myself. (There are persistent rumours of one still being out there, and there's a lot of excitement at unconfirmed reports.)

The extremists and the squabblers will get the publicity every time. Those who say feminism has been hijacked by prigs (nah, too big to be hijacked). One who says we mustn't sleep with men (nobody's asking you to watch, dear). Someone who claims one woman has set back feminism by twenty years (fat chance).

Most Australian feminists are simply going to school, holding down jobs, having kids, grateful for the Equal Opportunity Act, and wanting votes translated into child care, equal pay and the fight against domestic violence. We get used to hearing 'feminists say . . .' when we haven't said anything of the sort. We remember the suffragettes were considered way radical for wanting the vote, and we don't care if we're called radical for demanding equal rights.

The myriad variations on feminist belief all revolve around equality of opportunity and freedom of choice: choice to be a full-time parent, a rocket scientist, a labourer or a florist, and the freedom to be respected for any of those choices, man or woman. The squabbling between the celebrities and academic extremists is a sexier angle, the media equivalent of a scrag fight on the oval, but it's not the whole story.

The usual commentators can go on about it until they're bald in the face but it won't make it so. The women's rights movement isn't spoken for by any one person or clique, let alone mythical digger-baiting male-virtue-sullying devil-dancing loons who have gone a bit funny in the head about frocks.

Unless somebody's given me the wrong leaflet.

Uneasy Lies the Head That Wears the Big Tiara Thingie

We have a new Miss Universe, crowned this week in Namibia, HURRAH, and yes, the winner's name ends in an i – Chelsi Smith (Miss USA, actually, surprisingly enough). If she doesn't dot that i with a little smiley face I shall be very much saddened.

God, I love the Miss Universe contest. It is better than Miss World because, as the name suggests, people from other planets may enter, something that has become increasingly obvious over the years. The only thing wrong with last week's extravaganza is that is hasn't been on telly here yet: an indisputable OUTRAGE. If 600 million people around the world got to see Miss Venezuela's norks, why didn't we?

Beauty quests are very fabulous contributions to today's society for many reasons, and I shall touch on just some of these. They take our mind off sad things, not unlike a squirrel grip to the groin momentarily distracting us from thoughts of Arthur Tunstall. Quests are a charming reminder of our rustic past, like a mallet in a glass case tagged 'early anaesthetic' in a medical museum. In this way, they can be seen as a period drama.

Speaking of which, women who live or work in close proximity will begin to have synchronised menstrual cycles. I love the idea of the Miss Universe contestants all having PMT at the same time, preferably during the telecast. 'Miss Latvia, you are now level with Miss Tuvalu whose homeland boasts five sizeable lagoons! Your feelings?' (Choking sobs, Miss Latvia gestures offstage to hot water bottle wranglers.) 'Miss Australia, what are, what ARE your hobbies?' 'What's it to ya? I'm off to belt that cow Miss Liechtenstein right in the kisser.' (Miss Universe could only be improved by a scrag fight.)

Beauty contests (sorry, Pageants of Personality) have brought us much happiness and laughter. The single mother stripped of her title. The idea of wearing bathers and high heels at the same time. The rumour that each Miss Venezuela goes to the same cosmetic surgeon (and the more documentable phenomenon of Miss Venezuelas being constant finalists). The revival of the 'Get Smart' cone of silence, used when we are down to two babes (sorry, Women of Tomorrow): one goes into the cone of silence so she doesn't hear the tie-breaker question, which is usually something like, 'Do you believe in feminism, or the toothfairy, and how would you like to change the world?'.

During this question and the answer, which should involve the words 'dedicate myself', 'children', 'future', 'thank you' and 'free trade agreements' in no particular order, we have a chance to check out the contestants' boosies, back molars and fetlocks (sorry, poise, intelligence, and, oh, poise).

I always like the judges. These are usually experts in the field including Joan Collins, some gay actor who's still in a closet fitted with a tanning salon, and the very old, corpulent, gouty, unfortunately wigged managing directors of the sponsor companies.

The contestants (sorry, delegates) have a very difficult job: gluing those swimsuits to their buttocks, inventing new ways with spangles, and walking down steep stairways in stiletto heels, a long skirt and something huge, ornate and heavy on their head (such as their hair, for example).

The Miss Universe concept is holding up brilliantly. It's stupid; it's sexist; it's hilarious; it has tears, laughter, hairspray, sequins, smalltalk, surgery, song, scandal, baby elephants; it's a reminder that feminism hasn't gone too far: something for all the family.

In recent years, men have entered charity fundraising and suburban beauty quests, demanding equal opportunity. (And gee, they must be really hot dates, those guys, don't you think?) Well, if they must crash a tradition that was working perfectly, all right. As long as they come down the steep steps in high heels and bathers.

Pretty Implausible Woman

I can't be bothered writing a column. I can't be bothered getting up in the mornings (I can't even be bothered doing it in the afternoons). I can't be bothered getting on public transport to go to my full-time job and the only answer I can think of to 'Good morning, glorious pinnacle of darlingness' is 'You and whose berloody army, pal?'. Utter ennui, I've got.

Well, that's not entirely true. Sometimes, with enormous effort, I can rouse myself from the don't cares into a fierce quarrelsome pout of grumpiness, which I prefer to take out in unprovoked surliness on my remaining friends, some of whom are occasional furniture, and one of whom is a rubber hot water bottle, slightly perished.

July is the weepiest month. I'm over twenty-nine so it can't be the dreaded 27–28-year-old compulsory Spin Out and Soul-search (SOS) depression. I thought I might have clinical depression, but I'm still depressed even after I leave the clinic. Is it the bitterness of the dead (dead!) of winter? Is it the fact that if you stand at a bus stop the wind comes sideways at roughly 126,000 kilometres an hour, which means it was frotting round the Antarctic slightly earlier this morning, and then the very same wind goes right through you as if you are a cheese grater with a bit of tissue gaffer-taped to one side?

Finally, after three months, a bus comes. 'Where is this bus GOING?' you shriek. The driver, who probably has eighty-eight degrees in being a brain surgeon from her country of origin and never envisaged using her talents in quite this way, replies succinctly: 'I don't know!' 'Shut up and drive!' 'That'll be $2.10! I hate you!'.

What other response would be sensible, in this vindictive, atrophied season that has neither the aesthetic briskness of autumn or the sexy anticipation of spring? Lying rigid under the kitchen table and refusing to come out, that's what. Otherwise it's get up in weather a fairy penguin would grimace at, come home in the freezing dark and eat bits of sawdust in the broom cupboard.

I don't know where this is leading us. How about Hugh Grant and his girlfriend trying to 'work through' their relationship after his arrest for having sex in a car with a Hollywood street sex worker? Oh, all right. I have been involved in some sordid, triangular, pedestrian melodramas in my life but never quite so public or quite so involving of a pedestrian.

The New Face of Estee Lauder, Hugh's girlfriend Miss Elizabeth, might be understandably all puffed up from humiliation, betrayal and fury. (Perhaps the new slogan could be 'Give him a tongue-lashing without smudging yer lippy'.) It must be harder to be forgiving with eighty-seven Fleet Street cameras up your pooter every time you look out the window; forgetting is out of the question. Hughie already has been punished for getting caught. But at least he was only arrested once. How often has the sex worker, Divine Brown, been arrested doing something men want?

She's now got a chance to beat Julia Roberts's record for 'most implausible end to sex worker's career on Sunset Boulevard'. Sir Hugh may spend the rest of his life cringing when somebody says, 'Oh, that's divine, dwarling'. But maybe Ms Brown now has a chance to stop standing on street corners where chill winds go right through her, of hypocrisy (society demands your presence but we're going to call you a slut and arrest you) and media ennui (this is more interesting than Burma, chaps). If film stars get $2 mill a picture, Ms Brown deserves at least $1 mill for what her work must have been like. Take the money and run, Divine. Everybody else will.

Provoking Insights

'While rape or sexual harassment can never be condoned, it is true that some women dress or act provocatively so as to evoke a response. Civilised men learn to control themselves early on, but not all men are civilised, especially when drunk. It is about as sensible to expect such provocation always to be safe as to walk around some areas of New York with a wad of money sticking out of your pocket.' – *Sydney Morning Herald* and *Age* columnist Padriac McGuinness.

Now, some of you may think that Mr McGuinness is an immoderate old wanker who wouldn't know if there were three grand pianos up each nostril, but I think he has a point. In fact, I think his biggest mistake is not defining 'provocatively'. Allow me to assist.

Nuns' Habits
It is well known that nun outfits are among those most often requested of sex workers by their clients who require a fantasy along the lines of 'Mother Superior' or 'Yes, Sister, I have been a very naughty boy'. Nuns have a tendency to walk about the streets dressed in extremely nun-like habits. I rest my case.

School Uniforms
You would not believe the number of young women who get about in school uniforms, often carrying school bags and flaunting school socks – in many cases, deliberate pigtail involvement is suspected – despite the popularity of schoolgirl fantasies at any respectable brothel. Actually being required to be dressed as a schoolgirl because you are, in fact, a schoolgirl is hardly what could be described as a legitimate excuse for this sort of tarty get-up. 'The times I have been most forcefully groped in public were when I was dressed as a schoolgirl', comments Stephanie, 38, a jolly professional hockey player. 'Luckily I haven't been required to dress in this fashion for many years.'

Skirts
Enough said.

Trousers
Damned provocative, as any fool knows.

Low-cut Blouses
This particular kind of garment is just plain designed to make civilised men forget their civility training. (Men without shirts are not provocative because women take special tablets every morning to control their desires, which might otherwise get RIGHT OUT OF HAND.)

This other point that Mr McGuinness raised was a revelation to me: 'Civilised men learn to control themselves early on'. He also pointed out that 'some extreme wimminists . . . think that all men are rapists' (I don't know what a wimminist is, possibly a small marsupial in need of counselling). Mr McGuinness seems to agree with most of us that all men are not rapists, but only because the men who are not rapists are having to control themselves.

I have several men of my acquaintance, many of them certified darlings and a couple of whom I would trust with my life. To think that they are all actually seething would-be rapists, just hanging on to civilised behaviour by sheer willpower! 'Oh, absolutely, mate', confirmed Kev, 26, an attractive blond rotary hoe consultant. 'When I turned six, all us little boys were taken to special classes about how to be civilised even when drunk.

'There was an intensive workshop session on how you have to hold back from your natural urge to randomly sexually assault women even if they are asking for it, for example, by wearing an alluring tracksuit pants and parka ensemble. It's quite hard work, but, then, civilised behaviour has its price. Do you want to have a beer and go see a movie on Friday night?'

I don't know about you, but I reckon he's *asking* for it.

Up Yours Cazaly

Dear Wayne Carey

You're a brilliant Aussie Rules footy player, you boot beautiful goals, you look a bit gorgeous in those topless pin-up shots. But man, last week you depressed the hell out of us.

Last week you pleaded guilty to grabbing a stranger's breast at 9 a.m. on a Sunday in a city street, and saying 'Why don't you get a bigger set of tits?'. (They had to be bigger than your brain, Wayne.) It is understood that you had been out all night after your team, North Melbourne, was knocked out of the AFL finals series last year. You had left a nightclub with other players and were crossing the road when the assault occurred.

It ain't that you should go to jail for what you did, or even get a fine. But here's the thing: a lot of people would like you to really understand what you did and express heartfelt remorse about it – not because it resulted in bad publicity or salacious media headlines, but because what you did was scary, painful, humiliating and unacceptable to society. (That's why it's illegal, Wayne.)

I'm writing this because I wish the magistrate had said to you: 'Imagine you are a woman crossing the road with a friend at 9 a.m. on a Sunday, Mr Carey. Several very large, strong men come towards you in a group. Maybe they look pissed, or just pissed off. Unbelievably fit men, with huge shoulders, arms, hands and legs, packed with muscles from years of pumping iron and training hard. Oh jeez, several men built like Kelvinators coming right at you. One of the very big men grabs you by the breast. He says something insulting, something cruel. He hurts you physically.

'It doesn't occur to you to thank him for his kindly appraisal. This behaviour is so frightening, so unexpected, so out of line. You are in shock. You realise it might be dangerous to try to defend yourself. If a man does this to you, might he not also punch you in the jaw for no reason? Where will he grab you next? Is he drunk? Is he bonkers? He is certainly unpredictable. Will his mates join in? Try to imagine how you would feel, Mr Carey'.

Footballer promoter Ricky Nixon reckons footy players are now saying, 'We can't even go out at night any more'. He says, 'They've all got to reassess their social life and their activities after dark'. (Women, too, of course, have always had to assess their risks and be careful after dark. Not to mention 9 a.m. on a Sunday.)

One of your colleagues said, 'That sort of thing happens in nightclubs a hundred times a week. I'm not saying I condone it but I've been to other nightclubs, I've seen how other blokes act with women, but this bloke's been hung up for all to see'. (Your supporters said you were 'crucified', but I thought Gary Ablett was God.) After the court case you said you were sorry 'if' your actions had offended anyone. What's with the 'if'? Wouldn't you be offended if someone publicly got your goolies in a squirrel grip and said your willy was weeny? And what if you were terrified as well?

Next time North loses a final, maybe you should go home and have a Ribena. You were caught for doing something a real role model for little boys shouldn't do, and if other blokes do it in nightclubs, instead of outside, that's not okay either. You think all the publicity was unfair, uncalled for? Okay, but so was the assault. You say you don't remember it – she will.

There are many ways to be a big man, Wayne. One way is to be truly sorry and say it like you mean it. Another, as Aretha Franklin sings, is 'R.E.S.P.E.C.T. Find out what it means'.

Dealing with Heels

Earlier this column brought you a handy guide on how to dress sensibly and avoid rape (steer clear of nuns' outfits, school uniforms, skirts, trousers). Just before we get off the sexual assault train, we should have a dekko at the current fad of suggestions on how to deal with sexual assault or harassment.

Author Helen Garner has been putting in her three cents worth on all the radio and telly shows and in the papers, suggesting on the '4 Corners' program that a woman groped by a man could slap his face or stamp down hard on his foot with her high heels. (In the hypothetical case put to her, the older man is responsible for the young woman's university bursary money.)

Let's just examine this theory, shall we? We shall have to wear high heels at all times, just in case. This may slow down the swimming squad, and look kind of weird with jeans, but a glamorous rapid response has its price. (Imagine, girls, the social mortification of being caught short in flatties when a man squeezes your breasts! Blushorama!)

I'm tremendously excited by this idea. Just imagine the mighty morphin' power surge of tap-dancing around an office ready to act like Clint Eastwood in sequinned stilettos at any moment. (Don't forget to make a noise like Miss Piggy from 'The Muppets' when she does her little karate chops.)

Why, the word 'stiletto' itself comes from the Italian for 'dirty great knife thing'. Already there are teams of girly scientists testing the blunt instrument performance levels of the platform thong. And it's only a small step from cork soles to corked thigh. Be afraid, sleazy men of the world: these boots are made for whackin'.

Perhaps we might also consider the likely reactions of a man who is slapped. Imagine your work supervisor undoes the zip on your frock. You respond with a sharp right hook. I think he'll very probably respond quietly, 'Oh. Thank you very much Miss, I needed that. Take next week off'.

Or say you're seventeen and a teacher old enough to be your grandad monsters you in a lift and puts his tongue in your mouth. After a short, ugly struggle you slap him fair across the face. Will he a) give you a David Jones charge card with a three grand limit or b) burst into a supportive chorus of 'I Am Woman' and give you a good mark at the end of the year? (See if you can guess before you slap him.)

If, as Garner says, it is priggish and brutal for young women to take an alleged harassment or assault to court, after all other avenues have failed them, then women might consider ignoring the nasty old law altogether. (If somebody steals your car, you should go and speak sternly to them the next day. If they do it again you may write them a curt note. Trust me, I used to be an etiquette adviser.)

In the past, ladies were encouraged to swing the handbag or poke offenders firmly with a hatpin. In serious cases, one might lightly rake one's fan over his knuckles. One could also speak rather sternly to him, on the very good chance he would reply, 'I've been getting away with this for forty years, but if you *really* think so, I'll give it a rest'.

Obviously there are many guidelines for how to deal with the problem, but I think whacking the bloke around the chops is far more ladylike. If there's one thing this society needs, it's more one-on-one violence, vigilantism, and high heels. Well, okay, that's three things. We've got a long way to go.

9
Travels with My Id

A Real Trip

Travel writers do stuff. They bungy-jump, surf-ski, paraglide, haggle gaily with wizened peasants in the marketplace, take the midnight ferry, feel up a dolphin, eat battered eel willies, and still find time to thoroughly inspect the ruins.

Why don't they ever tell you what to do when you're on a business trip and all you get to see is the inside of hotel rooms and convention centres? Perhaps I can be of assistance, after my recent short tour of New Zealand.

Here, the many pesticide advertisements during the news indicate a rural nation. This is something you may only suspect because you flew over about 126 million sheep after your plane was delayed for three hours. Another clue: a judge is reported saying that the country's mental health system is run on a 'number 8 fencing wire mentality', and everyone understands this.

The in-house videos *Dripping Desire*, *Talk Dirty to Me* and *All the Right Motions*, all star somebody called Tracy, who it is promised will be shaking her booty. (Mostly her front booty.) 'The name of this movie will not appear on your bill', the TV tells you. (Your bill will say '$15.60 for one of those filthy pictures which we won't name but we're pretty sure had Tracy in it'.)

In New Zealand the popular soap opera is called 'Shortland Street', set in a hospital. Script lines include 'You're not in Guatemala now, Doctor Ropata', 'I'm innocent, I tell you!' and 'If you don't get in there now, the patient may die!'. Happily, this will soon be on SBS.

You may see a promo for a TV show, the highlight of which would be a 'wild goat recovery'. I missed the rest of this because somebody knocked on my door and asked me if I wanted my bed turned down. Clearly, there are weary travellers everywhere who gasp with relief, crying 'Yes, thank God you've come!'.

Your hotel room will also contain a beautifully bound, glossy coffee-table book you are not allowed to steal that shows all the things that are elsewhere in New Zealand. This includes stunning snow-capped mountains, bungy-jumping, drop-dead gorgeous waterfalls, canoeing, breath-taking hiking trails, cafe society, bubblingly excitable mud pools, bungy-jumping, misty mystical experiences with nature, and bungy-jumping. You may look at the pictures.

Do make friends with the concierge and room service. This will ensure that when you have visitors downstairs you do not want in your room (such as seventeen journalists) you may say, 'Is that you Carlos? Take them up to the roof and shoot them'. Carlos will say, 'Certainly madam', and Susan will send you up another hot chocolate (three marshmallows) to celebrate.

(New Zealanders are all so kind and helpful and friendly that even when you are an author and only one person has turned up for a book-signing they will say things like 'New Zealanders are shy' or 'Some of them were eaten by bears on the way to the shop'.)

New Zealand is roadtesting new cable channels, which gives you far greater flexibility. Channel 5, for example, shows a live picture of a clock. You can watch the second hand go around and listen to classical music. Channel 6 is a picture of a whiteboard with the number '6' written on it in blue felt pen. Channel 7 is the same as Channel 5, except you can listen to rock music.

P.S. If in Christchurch, do not say 'What a pretty little creek'. It is the mighty and thunderous, justly famous, beloved and revered River Avon. Thank you.

Don't Put Your Daughter on the Plane

The author visited London to promote her book *Real Gorgeous*, about body image and the beauty industry. Here are some searing excerpts from her diary.

Tuesday
6.15 a.m. Collected in a car from Channel 4 for 'The Big Breakfast', which my publicity department briefing notes explain is a 'talk with wacky Lily Savage (transvestite comedian!!!). Show is very popular, goes out daily (closest comparison 'Hey, Hey')'. Oh God. I was really looking forward to a talk about relaxed women's body image with a six-foot-three-inch tall bloke in drag who waxes his entire body, wears three-inch heels and a wig approximating the dimensions but none of the spiritual wonder of Uluru. Matters improved hugely when Lily introduced me live at 7.06 a.m. as a beauty expert.

Lily and I chatted for three segments in her 'beauty salon' with me giving advice to listeners' queries (actually the producers wrote them all). 'Tracey of Basingstoke's husband' wanted her to have plastic surgery so she could look like Sharon Stone. 'Leave your husband', I advised her. 'Oo-er!!!!' shouted everybody, including the crew. (It's that kind of *wacky* show. Six cameras and no way of knowing whether the one up your frock is transmitting.)

I learned that being a guest on a high-rating telly show is just about filling in the space. If you're lucky you get half an important message across, in my case the message was 'I am a gormless idiot'. Lucky nobody I know was watching except my cousins from Stoke Newington and half the theoretical physics department of London University. (I also learned that Lily is to star in a musical version of the Australian TV series 'Prisoner' with the original 'Freak'.)

Wednesday
9.45 a.m. While consulting the map to find out where VIVA! women's radio is, the publicist explains that its founder was the model for Edina on 'Absolutely Fabulous', and her daughter is the producer of the show I'm on. What might have been more useful, however, is the information she imparts later: the interviewer, Tara Newley, is the daughter of Joan Collins.

Teeny Tara, in a Chanel-style suit made out of the kind of tweedy, gaudy fabric they do for on-site caravan upholstery, was informed during a break that next week was Wonder Bra week! Tara was beside herself with joy. She *loves* her Wonder Bra. She *loves* the idea of wearing it to work one day next week. Who announced it was Wonder Bra week, I asked. The manufacturers of Wonder Bra!

Who would have thought!?

'What part of America are you from?' asks Tara politely. 'Ah. I'm actually from Australia', I apologised. 'Ha, ha', she laughs gaily. 'I've lived in so many places in the world ... California ... I just don't take any notice of accents anymore.' 'Ha, ha', I laughed gaily back, wanting to poke her twinkly eyes in and run screaming into the street.

This mob seemed to have all the wit and brain power of half a Ryvita wrapped in *Woman's Day*. If this is what happens at an all-women station, roll on Radio Bloke.

Thursday
10 a.m. Interview with the very bouncy Petroc Trelawny for London News Talk radio. I was expecting it to be like being interviewed by a Labrador puppy, but, astonishingly, he had looked at the book *and thought about the interview*. Blimey. I was going to make a joke about pet rocks, but I was sucking up to Petroc like mad and decided not to risk it. Publicity tours turn you into a toadying ninny. I was starting to offend myself.

1–4 p.m. Make-up and sitting around waiting for a ten-minute live appearance on SKY TV. My bit followed a man showing how to wrap up a chair with a big bow at the back and then an American singer who mentioned her child abuse and violent marriage in her three-minute interview and then came off and asked her publicist whether she looked fat on camera. The producer of my segment came and sat down in the waiting room and said the other producer was behaving like a right cow.

I went on and the host, a chilly, mean-eyed woman, white-blonde in a Tara suit, said she'd *love* a bit of computer-enhancing to make herself look thinner. (If she looked any thinner she'd be fettuccine.) While the camera was on me during our interview she gesticulated furiously and screeeeeamed silently at the floor manager, centimetres from my face, because the wrong cartoons kept coming up on the screen. It was kind of difficult to keep the thread of my sentences, and creepy the way she let her face fall back into feigned interest when the camera returned to her.

She then pitted me against the former 'Max Factor Girl', an ex-model who agreed with me entirely and revealed even more secret shenannigans in the magazine industry before she was cut off so that we could see four muscly men in silver holographic leotardy thingies called the Funk Phenomenon do something alarmingly cardiac.

I believe I may have made an idiot of myself again but at least I didn't wrap up a chair.

I have seen the future of cable telly and it is hours and hours of insincere presenters, distinguished only by their mediocrity, and wearing their very shallowness as a badge of nothing more than proximity to questionable celebrity. They will gallop through people and matters poignant or trivial with never a change in expression or emphasis. They should all be locked up. (Or maybe I was just hypoglycaemic.)

7 p.m. Literary evening. After a singularly Australian behind-the-scenes political stoush about whether she was literary enough to have her own evening (i.e. her books actually make money) Australia House hosted toast-mistress Kathy Lette, who, as I'm sure she herself might say under a waggling eyebrow, went down very well. Ms Lette, in a gorgeous suit, had boxes of books and a long line of well-wishers wanting her signature. Although I was, from memory, wearing long johns and thongs, or an army blanket or something, I could not slap her as she was far too nice to me. (In contrast, there were only five copies of my book in the building – at least they all sold.)

Our High Commissioner, a Mr Neal Blewett, displayed superior diplomatic skills by firmly kissing Ms Lette and me and propelling us to the door even more firmly with a very, very firm hand in the small of each authorial back. (I cannot overestimate the firmness of this.) At one stage we reached speeds of Mach 2 across the flash marble foyer. A very drunk Australian girl might have had photographic evidence of this efficient manoeuvre had she not lurched at the wrong time and snapped a bit of her own nostril.

Friday
9 a.m. I was in the shower when the phone rang. It was Radio Scotland wondering why I was not in the London BBC studio for a live cross to 'Thank God It's Friday!'. I explained I had been told that we would be thanking God for Friday at 9 in the *evening*. We would have to do the

interview live on the phone even though it was not their goddamn policy, dammit.

One of my most reliable sexual fantasies was warped forever as I stood wet and cold in the nuddy and entertained a man with a Glaswegian accent for a couple of minutes before we were smote apart forever by an ad for crunchy somethings. Would I never get this right?

Sunday

8 a.m. Collected from hotel for my appearance on the morning show of the new cable station Live TV. Courtesy car stopped for speeding. Upon arriving late, the producer peered grimacing into my face. 'You look . . . *tired!*' he says accusingly. 'And you'll have to do your own make-up.'

This was a shame because up until then the make-up woman usually asked more intelligent questions about one's book than the TV host. This show's host, who has dark brown skin to my light white, lent me what make-up she could. 'This lipstick's on crooked', I complained, batting at it with a tissue. 'Don't worry, your smile's crooked anyway', helped the publicist. Lovely.

The producer rushed in: 'I'm going to get you to do a couple of minutes on what's in the newspapers today'. I prepared a few pages to chat about. Just before the interview, he said, 'What are you going to say about Will Carling [rugby jock] and Princess Diana?'. 'Nothing.' 'WHAT? What about Emma Thompson and Kenneth Branagh breaking up? Relate that to fat, would you?'

'Um. I can't see how fat is relevant.'

'Fat, relate it to fat. Men, women, relationships, fat, everyone's the same, Ken and Em, fat.'

I started to think I was hallucinating. 'I really don't think I *can*.' He went *apoplectic*.

'THE THEME OF THIS WEEK', he thundered, 'IS RELATIONSHIPS!' He went to glower in the control room and the host introduced a clip from Emma Thompson's film *Carrington* first, which we could use to segue into RELATIONSHIPS and the newspapers. They rolled tape. It was *Apollo 13*. They stopped the tape. 'Gee, she looks good in an astronaut suit, doesn't she?' I said, risking a joke. The host looked at me, mystified. 'That was of course *Apollo 13*', she said to camera.

Because of this error, the papers segment went for ten whole minutes, while the producer hissed in Donna's ear to keep it on the subject of relationships. It went something like this.

Me: I see the French have blown the living bejeesus out of the Pacific again.
Host: Now to a more serious story. A swimming coach had relationships with the young women under his charge.
Me: Well, the charges of sexual assault would seem to show up a problem that can happen when young people are under the control of one adult, and desperate to retain their 'career', frightened to speak up. The 'guru' system can be dangerous . . .

Host: Yes, the *Daily Mail* seems to think Ken and Emma's marriage was broken up because of her success.
Me: Well, that's a bit unfair. I'm sure they've both been quite busy.
Host: And Ken's career has taken a very big dive recently.
Me: Look, I'm sure things will come right again for him: look at John Travolta.
Host: Who's he going out with?
Me: *Anyway*, the papers are all full of the Labour Party conference. I think you should call your papers 'The Blairs', every story is about Tony Blair and his new education policy.
Host: And Cherie Blair.
Me: Ye-e-es.

(And so on for about seven years.)

'God, it feels like you've been here for months', said somebody from the publishing company. Ye-e-es.

≈ZZZ≈

Jet Lag

Wilted, filleted and severely unsprounced from the glamour of international travel (I may well be dribbling on your shoulder, Sir, but it's nothing personal. Lighten up. Wow, look at that: who knew that ankles could swell up to approximate a king-sized futon? Mmm, airline breakfast – I'll need a statutory declaration if you're calling that a sausage, madam) I stumbled onto Australian Tarmac last week with inarticulate cries of gratitude.

Luckily, my paramour, Des Tiny, had arrived in the terminal (what an appropriate term) with a romantic gesture: a brass band quartet with triple tuba and a French horn heavy on the oom in oom pah pah played the hits of Nancy Sinatra in the terminal, as one was frisked by a customs officer who mistook one's ankles for two suitcases of cocaine and a concealed penguin colony. One bribed him with a boiled lolly and fell into the arms of Mr Tiny. Swoooon!

It later transpired through a gauzy, Joan Collins lens-like haze, that Des had been dismissed from Mistress Beverley's House of Wiglets and Wimples for advising a customer to perm his nostril hair. 'I am the avant garde', explained Des. 'And unemployed. Perhaps Rupert Murdoch has my best interests at heart. It is surely time that worldwide cable television had a new show, "Roots of the Stars", with me, Des "Toupees Ahoy" Tiny, the gracious host, interviewing celebrities such as Burt Lancaster and Rosemary Margan, follicle-wise.' Sadly, Mr Murdoch did not call. Which is just as well, considering that probably Mr Lancaster has held relatively few views on matters tonsorial since he carked it.

So when we went to our aerobic step synchronised water ballet workshops and Letitia Grungecozzie nearly drowned after a particularly ribald pas-de-trois with Heather Golightly and 'Hungry' Allenbaum, when her nasal plugs imploded, her subsequent comment made while being given the kiss of life by wildly reliable and attractive ambulance officers, 'My life flashed before my eyes and it wasn't all that interesting', gave Des and me a brainy wave, vis-à-vis a change of career for him.

From Thursday, the Des Tiny Interesting Past Invention Agency will fling open its tulip-shaped doors to a panting public. Want to be the love child of Percy Sledge and Sonia McMahon? No worries: facts mean nowt to us. (After all, truth is in the eye of the beholder: who would you believe, a bunch of bally foreign Papuan tribespeople at Ok Tedi saying a big mine has made their life hell, or giant old BHP with a humungous publicity budget? It's a tough one!)

Wish people thought you were asked to leave the French Foreign Legion because you were too stoic and it was frightening the officers? Convinced you'd seem more attractive if you once stormed the French consulate in a small Zodiac shouting, 'Chirac you barmy bugger, come out and fight like a homme!'? Can do.

We'll forge your brain surgery qualifications, register your appointment as Cuban cabinet minister, write you love letters from Peter Reith (no, all right, sorry) and doctor up photographs of you and Princess Diana playing Twister. Degrees from Oxford, Cambridge, Yale and the Southern Baptist School of Tantric Howsyourfather can be tricked up with some nice calligraphy and a biggish pink ribbon.

There'll be a special interview service, in which we provide a tape of your live interview with Bobby Batista on CNN after rescuing the hostages; or explaining to Oprah when you first realised you might be heterosexual; or being on 'Burke's Backyard' showing him through the first three acres of virgin woodland with inground pool. We can provide signed photographs with sentimental and ostentatious thanks from Ronald Biggs, Patti Newton, Hughie Newton, Patti Labelle, Paul Keating, the Queen Mother and Big Bird.

You need never feel inadequate again with a letter from Gary Ablett/Magic Johnson/Madam Lash in your kick saying, 'Thanks for teaching me everything I know about the game. Yours, ever'. Forget all this nonsense about past lives, make this one more interesting, retrospectively. You have nothing to lose but your past!

Hayseed Holiday Hints

As the holiday season is bearing down upon us like a road train driven by a maniac on amphetamines, it may help to pass along some hints about country life, in case you go bush instead of beach this summer. (Some questions, of course, remain unanswered, such as 'Why does it smell like squished ants after it has been raining?' and 'When did the hay fashion police decide that rectangular hay bales are OUT and rolled up hay bales are IN?'.) Our research has revealed the following.

Geographical Features
Near where you are staying in the country will be several points of interest. In our case last week, about halfway between Sydney and Melbourne, these were called Mount Misery, Mount Buggery, Mount Disappointment and The Pimple. (Seriously.) It's just an inkling, but personally I would have preferred Mount Hurrah Hurrah Hurrah, Mount Foreplay, Mount Utterly Thrilling Fabulousness and The Attractive Knollish Thing.

If you find yourself in a rural area, try not to be put off by these names. It's just that a whole lot of colonial explorers went poncing around the place, got massacred by mozzies, found they couldn't get any tea and scones and there was always an echidna in their swag, and they got very grumpy indeed.

Because of this, Australia is now covered in places called Extremely Peeved Ridge and The Whinging Islands. Luckily very few pale women were allowed to explore things then, or we'd be attempting to picnic on Mount Pre-Menstrual Tension Everything Is Doomed Aaaarrrgh Who Do You Think You Are Sunshine, Hume Or Hovell And What Do You Mean You Forgot The Chocolate.

Cicadas

Cicadas are very lovely insecty God's creature things who rub together their wings or legs or jowls or something and make a joyous noise as part of life's rich tapestry of natural wonders. They do this in roving packs of up to three trillion right outside the door and everywhere else in the vicinity from first light until 8.30 p.m., until your eardrums vibrate at exactly the frequency of insanity. If there were cicadas like this in the city the debate about aircraft noise or wheel-clamping would be forgotten as people roamed the streets blasting anything that chirrups.

Fauna

In the country, there are cows. It is the cows' job to stand around in paddocks and poop a lot. Sometimes the cows will all face the same direction. Sometimes they will face in different directions, if there's been a cow contretemps. Every now and then a cow will feel the need to go moo, and this is usually expressed thusly, in a rising inflection: 'Mghooooooough'. They are distinguished from sheep by the fact that sheep go 'Mbbwaaaaaaagh' and are generally woollier in appearance. The taller ones are horses.

There are also bandicoots, echidnas, chooks, kangaroos, farm dogs and brown snakes. Birdlifewise, you've got your kookaburras who go 'Woohahahaha' and little wrens who keep their thoughts pretty much to themselves.

Waving
When you are driving in the country, wave to other drivers you pass on the road. None of your Queenie sort of wrist-rotator waves, or demonstrative arm waving, thank you. Without altering your very serious driving expression, simply raise your hand from the steering wheel in a discreetly languid salute. If you are a bit weary, an index finger is acceptable.

The wave is shorthand for: 'I am waving at you because we are in the country. If we were in the city I would ignore you, or push you under a train, or lean on my horn until you get out and threatened my person. But we are in the country, and therefore, we wave. I haven't a clue who you are, but I'm waving. Hello, we're in the country'. Continue doing this until you approach the increased traffic of the big smoke and your hand becomes paralysed.

Travels with My Id

C'mon Baby, Do the Aviation

It started snowing in Manhattan. 'Sorry,' I explained to the mavens in the cultural eye of the storm, 'I have to go to the Mallacoota Arts Festival.' 'No worries', replied Robert de Niro, or maybe it was Dustin Hoffman. 'Give my regards to Broadway. Trevor Broadway.'

Obviously, it was time to get on the plane. I don't know if you do much travelling by aeroplane, but I have done far too much of it for work lately, and I have a few hints for you. People make jokes about the airline food, but really, things have changed. And I don't think you can laugh at airline food any more. No, you can sob, maybe, or go up and bang on the cockpit door. 'You in the braid! What do you call this then? Hey, Joystick Boy! In exactly what way does this object resemble a sausage?' (The Trade Practices Commission needs to look at this. 'Airline food', as a concept, would seem to imply something edible.)

'Airline food' actually indicates 'Plastic fork plus coloured chemicals. Also maybe some little, hard, round orange things'. On one flight, the guy next to me said to a flight attendant, 'Excuse me, miss, what is this?' She regarded the plastic tray solemnly. She opened her mouth, closed it, cocked her head and put a finger to her chin. She went away to consult with a colleague. She came back. 'Apparently it's lunch, sir.' It brings new meaning to the phrase 'hollow laugh'.

Actually there was no need to bang on the cockpit door during one flight from Los Angeles to Chicago, where winds gusting up to seventy-eight zillion miles an hour had closed almost all the runways. We were kept on the Tarmac for about two and a half hours before finally taking off. As a gesture of pointedly positive public relations, the pilot, in a snazzy uniform and peaked cap like a doorman's, took a stroll down the aisle, and chatted languidly with the irate passengers. 'Hey. Hi there. How you doin', champ! Like my epaulettes?'

Now, this in itself was a charming idea. It's just that I wish he'd done it after the plane landed. Not DURING the flight. People were saying to him, 'Hey man, I'm gonna miss my connection!' I was just thinking: 'WHAT ARE YOU DOING HERE! OY! Does the concept "Both hands on the WHEEL" ring any bells?' We landed safely in Chicago. 'Nice landing', I said to the chatty pilot, who was saying bye-byes at the door. 'Yurp. Neato. The co-pilot's job.' I don't know what they pay this guy for. Maybe he sits on the co-pilot's knees and steers when they get out in the country.

A big part of the miracle of modern aviation is that no matter what flight you are on in what country, London to Singapore, Chicago to New York, or Auckland to Melbourne, the alleged 'in-flight entertainment system' (hello, Trade Practices Commission?) will be showing a movie called *The American President*. This is so that viewers don't get confused thinking that Hollywood might have cast Michael Douglas as the sexy president of Azerbaijan, or of Burkina Faso. I have been present at nine screenings of this movie. It's better without sound. And quite nice if you close your eyes.

Another thing to know about air travel is how small the toilets are and how big the wattage of the lighting. After twenty-four hours of flight, going to the toilet in a plane is like standing in a matchbox with a light bank from the night footy up your left nostril. I found a hair on my face I had never noticed before in the aircraft toilets, and the hair was about seven metres long. 'Why didn't you TELL me?' I asked the pilot. 'I was too busy trying to work out if this thing is a sausage', he said.

Helena Handbasket

There's nothing like returning from holiday to find that everything has gone to hell in a handbasket or, as I used to think it was, gone to Helena Handbasket, who must be really quite despondent by now.

Firstly, frightful and terrible things have happened in Port Arthur, and now it appears that there are actually a relatively weeny number of people in this country who believe that it should be legal to own semi-automatic weapons.

At this point it may be a bit late to enter the debate as no doubt everything has been said including 'Shut up at the back or we'll pop you all in the pokey', but in lieu of decent gun laws I would like to make a small suggestion for the semi-automatic weapon application form. Question One: do you want to own a semi-automatic gun? If Question One is answered in the affirmative, then the person may be judged possibly a bit unsuitable to own one, so, no. And if the person answers, 'No, I don't want a semi-automatic gun; I am trying to register my Jack Russell terrier, Mr Whiskers, with the council', this matter can be attended to.

Or not. Local councils are not necessarily where things are properly attended to. I have just received a letter from the local council that is a reply to my request to waive a visitor's parking fine, because somebody else had driven off with my visitors' permit. Well, the council letter takes seven paragraphs to tell me basically a) get rooted, b) the fine has just been increased by $13.90 and c) *'No further correspondence will be entered into*. Yours faithfully, Mrs Cripola, Parking Administration'. (My italics.)

In the desperate hope that MRS CRIPOLA might see this wrapped around her souvlaki take-away: Dear MRS CRIPOLA. Is the point of parking rules in my street to allow only residents and their visitors to park in the permit zone? Or is the point of parking rules that the council can make money and charge people $13.90 for writing them a rude letter? How can you put your rubber-stamped name (or, your husband's, actually, by the look of it – good move) to it?

P.S. Your letter informs that two weeks ago I had two options – pay up or go to court. If I didn't pay up by two weeks ago (when I was in a small town near Turkey's border with Syria) you will assume I have 'elect[ed] to appear in court where the matter can be dealt with, thereby incurring further costs'. I did not so elect, but I can't even write to explain because you refuse to read my letters. MRS CRIPOLA, I will send you a cheque and hope for the best, but I shall never forgive you. Imagine all the former gun enthusiasts I'd meet in the slammer.

This of course is nothing compared to the trials of my Beauty Therapiste, Miss Francine Panto, of Francine's New Hairy Haven and Sprauncing Salon. Her builder, who claimed to be a member of the Housing Industry Association (liar, liar, his pants were on fire) refused to finish the job because it was 'taking up too much of his time' and advised her to 'buy the doorknobs yourself and poke them in'.

She likewise refused to pay him the rest of the agreed money and last night 'somebody' broke in and stole all her newly fitted doors from the Jooshing Parlour, the Plucking Nook and the Waxing Chamber (with soundproofing only half done in the screaming section) as well as all the cupboard doors in every room. Our Francine is precisely the sort of person who shouldn't have access to anything semi-automatic except a curling wand just at the moment.

10
Blathering On

Warning: Warnings

Have you noticed how you can hardly move these days for warnings? You've got your strong wind warning west of the coast of Wilson's Promontory. Your 'Do not take overturning vehicle' warning, sometimes difficult to see because of all the other signage on the back of your truck, including your silhouette of a naked woman, so essential to your long-distance haulage as a concept.

You've got your Hazchem warnings outside of buildings, in a special code so that the firefighters will know what they have to deal with. The code is important, because you wouldn't feel very warm and fuzzy about working in a building that had a dirty great sign out the front saying 'This building is riddled with unbeleeeevably inflammable toxic chemical by-products that when turned into smoke will strip the inside of your nostrils, make your skin turn inside out and render you a closet hyperventilator to the end of your days'. Something like WF^7#@ is far more reassuring to the general public and allows your firefighter to look up the little red book and go, 'Rats'.

Then you've got your gruesome car crash ads, and your ads called 'Look Up and Live', which is all about the very sound concept of not getting electrocuted. There used to be a telly ad in which a small person was about to stick a metal thingie in a power point and the Dad person in the ad leapt across the table in slow motion. It was absolutely terrifying and certainly did the job: there's no way I'm having kids if that's the sort of caper they get up to.

Warnings have become so ubiquitous that their authors have stopped prevaricating and become downright rude. The Victorian Traffic Accident Commission comes right out and says 'If you drink and drive you're a bloody idiot', whereas previously, this sort of information was usually provided by uncles, along with 'You'll need penicillin for that kind of thing, son' and 'Shut up and get a bloody job'.

The Austext service on Channel 7 provides several warnings along the bottom of the screen for people who have dialled up which roads to avoid on the way to work. These warnings include 'Make sure everyone in the car is belted up'. (In Melbourne you could drive them to a King Street nightclub and make them taunt bouncers. In Sydney you could try going to the Bondi Hotel and insulting somebody's sister.) Another helpful piece of instruction is 'Be courteous, friendly, and help other road users.'

This struck me as somewhat bizarre. What, precisely, is the point of advising somebody to be friendly? If the person is already friendly, it would appear to be redundant. If somebody is a cruel, ugly-minded social hand grenade who preys on the shy and slow-witted, will they change their ways? It reminds me of a friend who returned from a trip to the United States, shaking her head and muttering.

She had been watching American television and a community service ad came on, reminding parents a) it was perfectly acceptable to hug their kids and b) it wasn't a bad idea to feed them every day either.

It seems to me that these people who make slogans about the roads have not fully extended themselves. How about 'Just try not to run over anybody, would you?', 'Car should be stationary when you are changing a tyre' and 'That other big, round thing is the steering wheel'? Not to mention that 'Look right, look left, look right again and try to avoid Susan Renouf' could be handy.

Of course, there's no reason to restrict this sort of thing to road safety campaigns. Little reminders and warnings can be employed at every turn in the waking moments. 'Look out, Peter Reith's talking about the economy' and 'Do try to keep a straight face when Gareth Evans talks about East Timor' would be good. And I think we need some more generic messages to flash at us from screens and billboards everywhere. It can't be long until we see 'It is inadvisable to hurl yourself off quite tall buildings', 'Your underpants are NOT worn over your trousers' and 'Don't poke a tuning fork in your eye!'.

Don't say I didn't warn you.

A Slew of Collective Nouns

Two of my favourite characters on telly (if you don't count everything on 'Big Girl's Blouse') are Bubble, the personal assistant on 'Absolutely Fabulous', and Dominica, the receptionist at 'Frontline'. Complete airheads, the pair of them. They are also fictional, which, while recently accepted as a synonym for Demidenko, actually means ooterly made oop, as Bubble might say.

Real personal assistants and secretaries tend to be razor-sharp minds who can cut you off in a terwinkling. They know more about the boss than the boss does. It's a feeble-minded person indeed who insults a secretary. Or Germaine Greer. In Germaine's case you will be so comprehensively and gleefully insulted that you'll have to go and live in Penguin, Tasmania, whereas if you insult a personal assistant your calls will be sent to call-waiting-limbo-Greensleeves land forever and ever, thank you that line's still busy.

These assistants can make 'I'll get her to call you' sound like 'Over my dead body, creepy-pants'.

I knew an editor once who used to take luncheon until he could hardly stand. His expense accounts looked like a phone book and his name was on the masthead of a specialist magazine. His 'secretary', in between answering the phone, commissioning pieces, organising payments and editing the articles, would decide on the magazine's direction and focus. Occasionally the boss would pop in to check the size of his name on the masthead and complain about the entrée.

This is the long way of getting to the task at hand: we need some new collective nouns around the place, beginning with 'a power of secretaries'. You may already have come across the weird but true ones: a parliament of owls; an unkindness of ravens; an exultation of larks; a siege of bitterns; a charm of goldfinches; a clamour of rooks, and a murder of crows. (Not to mention an hallucination of ornithologists, by the sound of it.)

A purge of politicians
An exhortation of agents
A rout of rakes
A dilbrey of duffers
A shiver of thrillers
A drift of ex-husbands
A wander of ex-wives
A demand of toddlers
An insanity of bank charges
A pessary of doctors

A bounce of Baywatch babes
A seldom of actors
A palaver of columnists
A fad of focaccias
A cafe of lattes
A wedgie of underpants
A hoon of drunks
A prickle of gossips
An affront of comedians
A feely of sleazes

A cuppa of friends
A sloth of videos
A breakfast of champions
A pixel of computer programmers
A pander of producers
A fuss of grandparents
A gurgle of babies
A giggle of girlies
A swagger of blokes
A profit of mining executives

A flop of Kevin Costner films
A booty of boys
A flounce of supermodels
An allegation of journalists
A clench of fundamentalist Christians
A porkie of politicians
A crowing of Keatings

A scathing of Kennetts
A sooth of Kernots
An embarrassment of Richos

A perv of spectators
A hunk of lifesavers
A fanfaronade of lawyers
A froth of fashion designers
A minion of press secretaries
A pout of punters
A handknit of dopey ferals
A doh! of mistakes
A smirk of socialites
A leather pant of lead guitarists

Hello, Hello, Hello

I'm sure it won't happen to you, but just in case, let me tell you how to handle a burglary. Okay, first you come home, and you talk to a couple of friends on the phone, and then you decide to water the garden, right, and then you notice that somebody appears to have driven a combine harvester through the back door.

You walk back through your house and you find the only decent jewellery you ever had, gorn. Just gorn. And the camera. What does a thief want with a receptacle for five-month-old holiday snaps of my friends with cigarette papers stuck to their heads, playing 'Celebrity'? (It rained. We don't usually stick papers on our heads unless it rains or something.)

So you get the phone. 'Your Local Police, Senior Constable Doobrey.'

'Yes. Hello, Constable Doobrey. I've been burgled, or something. I mean, the back door is busted in. And stuff is gone.'

'Name, please . . . Oh, don't you write for that newspaper? The one that doesn't like the police?'

'Constable Doobrey, pur-lease. The newspaper loves the police. Journalists always suck up to the police. ADORE THE POLICE.'

'Ah, that's right, it doesn't like Jeff Kennett.'

'Just send a bloody car round, would you?'

'Righto', says a cheerful Constable Doobrey. Wise Constable Doobrey, excellent, probably extremely handsome, SENIOR Constable Doobrey.

Stalwart Constable Bun and Senior Constable Dimples will arrive, shortly after several friends who put on the kettle in relays. The police radio calls Senior Constable Dimples. 'Attending a cold burg', he replies. 'We'll call back.' Senior Constable Dimples will agree that, unlike tea, a cold burg is infinitely more satisfactory for all concerned than a lukewarm burg, and makes several excellent suggestions to you, one of which sticks in your mind: 'Get some insurance'.

It will be generally agreed that there is no point getting out the fingerprint kit, although it would pep up proceedings no end, because there will be seven million fingerprints on the back door since last week's Trash The Nasturtiums party. ('CIB will give you a burl tomorrow' means that some men in suits will be in touch by telephonics, apparently.)

Okay, at this stage you can look in the *Yellow Pages* and get Ross and Frank to come round in a car they borrowed from Steptoe and Son and nail a bit of tin on your back door for $100 cash, with four six-inch nails securing the back gate to the fence thrown in, utterly gratis. Ross will hit his thumb with the hammer, and Ross and Frank will fall about in hysterics when they hear the other quotes you got for the job.

Ross and Frank will be so entertaining, and do so well at choosing the right size bit of tin and nailing it onto the right door, that you will want to give them one of the bottles of champagne left over from the Nasturtium Fiasco but when you open the fridge, you will find that all the leftover grog has been nicked as well. Incidentally, Ross and Frank, by this stage, will be holding their sides. After they hear that there is no insurance, they will barely pull themselves together to write the invoice.

The next day, a deadpan CIB man will visit, claiming to be from Amway. The CIB will fail to lift any prints off the back door or the fridge, although they will get the lid off a jar of pickled squid you couldn't budge yourself, even though the CIB thinks it smells funny. Also, the CIB will ask your opinion of *The Beauty Myth*, and you should have something ready other than 'It didn't have enough pictures'. The CIB may also cast aspersions on the pink velour rabbit your mother gave you when you were two.

That's the trouble with burglaries: it's a real invasion.

Cats Suck

I wish to kill cats. I am not just suggesting, of course, that I be able to go forth into the streets armed with a blunderbuss, banging away at the sight of anything in tatty fur (certainly not in Toorak or Double Bay, or there could be errors such as those seen during duck season, which are usually explained by 'I mistook Ken, officer, for a small freckled muscovy').

As much fun as I could have indiscriminately blowing away cats, I am prepared to modify my wishes in accordance with society's rules. That is, I will only lay down some tracing fire and Scud activity in my own backyard. It is the passive cat ownership that is driving me crazy. If passive smoking is a vile social habit, why can't I shoot cats that enter my (sorry) 'personal space'?

I don't want cats. I don't like them. I am allergic to them. Cats are sly and weird and display all the most venal traits of human nature. They drop furry bits that make me sneeze. When they cough up fur balls they make a noise that would frighten an experienced mother of three. Cats are awful. And they always want to sit on me, which is a privilege I accord to very few people, even.

At this point cat owners will be claiming that cats are great company (yeah, right: how many *men* would get away with rubbing against your leg, saying 'Where's my dinner?' and then going out all night?). Or cat owners will say, 'I love my cat'. That's okay, but can't you do it in the privacy of your own home?

The only really ugly argument will come when a cat owner says, 'Oh, but cats are so clean. They are always cleaning themselves and they never soil their own area'. THIS IS BECAUSE THEY ARE COMING TO MY HOUSE AND POOING ALL OVER IT. They are digging up my daffodils and depositing their doo-doo. They are weeing from the nasturtiums to the tiny babies' tears, a poignantly named formerly green mossy expanse now reduced to something like an Agent Orange demonstration. When they're not vivisecting indigenous birdlife or trying to scratch each other's eyes out under my window at 3 a.m., your clean cats with delicate sensibilities are pooing their guts out on my roof.

And where is the legislation covering this passive cat ownership? This threat to public health is virtually ignored by all Equal Opportunity boards (where they are still permitted to operate with an annual budget of more than $2.50). This leaves only one course open to me, known as crazed vigilantism. I have been speaking with nursery staff and small arms experts and reading *Soldier of Fortune* magazine's small print advertisements, and I believe that I am ready to give you cat owners fair warning.

I have spiked some garden pots with pointy skewers. I will be placing chicken wire on other parts, which will of course greatly enhance the aesthetics. I have been refused permission for a handgun permit, which may be because I frothed slightly at the interview, took the constable by the lapels and shouted, 'Death to the furry! Ha ha aha ha aha aha ha. Ha'. Apparently I am still eligible for a semi-automatic weapon by mail order in Montana but that will take too long.

I'm going to be out there with a super-soaker water pistol, and when I hear the stupid tinkle of their stupid little bells, and see the reds of their mean little eyes, I am going to let your darling moggies have it right between their mean-spirited little whiskers.

Gratuitous Koala Bashing

Should we have a word about the environment? 'Cactus' would be a good one, or 'Whoopsie'. No, it's too depressing. The very concept of an environment fills me with despair and makes me want to press ice to my eyelids, which is also a Hollywood handy hint for puffy eyes caused by hard living.

Cutting down on the hard living is another option, as is cutting down all the trees. The environment debate seems to consist of a Government Minister saying, 'You think this is bad, the Opposition would raze the nation's shrubbery and strip-mine an area the size of, um, Australia'. The Opposition Shadow Minister usually replies, 'We would not, nerny, nerny ner, go on, hold and election I dare ya, go on, see if I care, made you look, ya dirty chook'.

The Prime Minister will say that all greenies are flaming hairy wackos and the foresters need a good lie down and the Opposition's secret policy is to support compulsory oil slicks and get the little kids to set it all on fire for a school project so why don't you all get rooted if you like trees, chum, life is a bowl of cherries and the Opposition is a bunch of pansies. Only I won't hear any of it because as soon as that man gets his laughing gear into a syllable I fall insensible to the floor and have a kip.

A tour of the local shopping precinct seemed to be the way to cheer right up. On the hard living front a beauty salon was offering an 'bio-molecular recovery treatment'. I inquired. 'It's a facial', said the woman, trying to keep a straight one.

I made my way to look at what Germaine Greer might call 'follow me home and make me some dinner, big boy' shoes, of the low-heeled variety. (At this point I should add that my shoes do not make a political or sexual statement. It's just that high heels have me tottering and lurching into people's laps on public transport, which does nothing for a girl's sober reputation, especially before elevenses.)

At the door of the pump parlour a very, very frightening thing happened. Like something out of a Stephen King novel, or a National Party family policy. A huge, skinny, saggy, mangy, shuffling, vile creature – dressed either as a dimwitted koala or a grey chenille bedspread that needs to be sedated – hurled itself in front of me shaking a yellow bucket with a Wilderness Society sticker on it. This hideous monstrosity apparently was soliciting funds, either to protect the wilderness or buy itself a bedspread with all tufts intact.

My intense fear and vicious loathing of furry costumes stems from an incident in my childhood at a school fete when a man in a bear suit, his sight impeded, punched me in the eye, knocked me to the ground, and then kept touching and hugging me and trying to find out if my parents were lawyers. This terror (of my parents being lawyers) has never entirely left me, and still surfaces whenever I am within whacking range of an occupied furry suit.

Wilderness Society be warned: if I see another one of those offensively unstylish koalas in my way I'm going to bio-molecularly re-arrange its face. If an environmental group is to be taken seriously, and bits of the planet are radioactive, then there is work to be done. I'm sending you a donation on the proviso that the koalas get the shunt. For heaven's sake take a long hard look at your public image: stop hanging around looking furry and floppy. It's never worked for Gareth Evans.

Just Testing

The other day a psychological study was in the paper, about a group of baby monkeys who were completely isolated to deprive them of physical affection. From what details I can recall, while I'm trying not to recall the study at all because it's so hideous, the baby monkeys died, or went off their rockers. Anyway, it didn't do them any good at all.

It's a bit on the haunting side, innit? What happened to the monkeys at the end of the study? What happened to their parents? Who paid for this? What are we supposed to do about the results: warn people not to ignore their monkeys? Were the behavioural scientists who devised it the same people who went round school giving the shy kids a Chinese burn and hurling their playlunch up their pants? (Surely we need a study on this.)

Apart from the obvious fact that the scientists ought to be taken down the back paddock and roughed up, the results of the monkey study seemed to be that if you never got a kind word or a cuddle you might go mad as billyo. Well, der. Of course it is already known that contact sport was invented by a bevy of Cro-magnon men who wanted an excuse to compliment each other and have a snuggle, however brief and manly, after the game.

I know this because a team of scientists interviewed 114 men from Iowa last summer and extrapolated the results into the past using a long-range sensitive sprauncometer technique invented by Dr Humber Vogue (Harvard), who was given the Nobel Prize for the Most Obvious Conclusion Possible in the Known Universe to Any Given Experiment in 1934, 1948 and 1949 (in a dazzling move, he entered the same conclusion two years running, viz, 'If you lie down with dawgs you get up with ferleas'. He proved this by extensive consultative work with his retriever, Shep.)

I say we get a representative team of behavioural scientists together and lock them in separate rooms with only a picture of a dried sardine each. For seventeen months they are to be denied any form of physical, emotional or sexual contact. At random moments one of the actors from 'Gladiators' will stick a head in the door and shout, 'Bang!'. Some of us here at the Institute of Big Fat Grants have an inkling that this might make the behavioural scientists kind of cranky, but we think it's best to be sure, scientifically.

The 'control' group, that is, the ones who will *not* be psychologically tortured, and I think for logic's sake these should be monkeys, guinea pigs, or probably us, should be provided with a very long holiday to a princessy sort of hotel in the Bahamas and given strawberries, daiquiris, chocolate, massage, optional snorkelling lessons and skilful French-kissing (well you can't boycott everything). At the end of the seventeen months we shall carefully evaluate whether we feel at all cheery.

Luckily we will hardly need to explain that a scientific study has authority because it is conducted by scientists. Some of them even have their own clipboards. You can already see this in advertising: 'Laboratory tests prove that you will get you a lot more sex if you use this toothpaste'. It certainly worked for the lab assistant, Jeremy. Of course, he actually had the more sex with himself, but there's no space on the form to write that down.

Shortly we will be turning our attention to 'Threats to Break a Bloke's Femur with a Shifting Spanner as Possible Predisposer to Rejecting Football as a Career' and 'Jumping Out from behind the Gate and Hosing Down the Neighbours on Windy Winter Mornings and Its Effect on Street Harmony: a Preliminary Survey'.

To Boldly Go on the Blink

Did you know that another space mission has gone completely berko? First the Hubble telescope gets sent up there and is about as much use as a pair of those X-ray specs you can get by filling in a coupon at the back of a comic. (The Hubble telescope, you will recall, cost three billion dollars, and was, um, out of focus.)

This was unrelated to the Chinese satellite that exploded into smithereens two minutes after take-off this year. Which wasn't the same Chinese satellite as the one that leaked and didn't get to where it was supposed to, launched earlier.

No, that wasn't the Optus satellite launched by China in 1992 that also exploded. And it was entirely unrelated to the incident in which NASA scientists found out that the space shuttle Discovery had a main engine pump that had bits attached by a subcontractor with Superglue. Or the piece of rocket that blew off and landed in the rose garden of the White House and killed the Clintons' cat. (Well, all right, I made that last one up, but I had you going there for a moment.)

Now the Galileo space craft 'has developed yet another potentially major communications problem that may seriously impair its ability to transmit images of the giant planet'. (The giant planet being Jupiter, which the bung space craft took SIX YEARS to get to, and now this.)

It's like blasting a Beta video recorder into space with a manual written in Urdu and a VHS Raquel Welch exercise tape. It's like trying to strain tea with a rhinoceros. It's like trying to explain the concept of compassion to a Victorian health minister. It is a complete bloody waste of time.

Galileo's antenna won't go up. The camera shutter won't stop opening and closing constantly. And now, 'ground engineers are struggling to work out why a tape recorder on board has ignored a command to stop rewinding', says a news report. (Listen, if I could get a six-year-old tape recorder to START rewinding I'd be throwing a daiquiri party.)

Still, the engineers must be going out of their scones. If only they were up there, with the tape recorder. They could swear. They could get the tape out and, using a lead pencil, wind the tape out of the cassette until it lies in long loopy strands on the floor, and then kick the tape recorder. If this didn't work, they could look at the instructions, find the guarantee in the sock drawer and realise that the machine has to go back into the plant while awaiting the parts, which will be sent from Venus and are expected to arrive some time the next century. That's how it works on Earth, anyway.

Galileo cost $680 million. So we can get some snaps of Jupiter. Or not. Certainly this must be covering the wages of NASA's Jet Propulsion Lab spokesperson, Mr William O'Neil, who said the spacecraft would now maybe only send 35 per cent of the information the scientists are panting for, here on Earth. Well, America. 'We'll have to invent a new way to get images back', he added, thinking perhaps of telepathy, or perhaps a really good courier service.

The Galileo will still be able to send other data back about Jupiter, say, little messages like 'Gee, it sure is dark out here', 'Wow, it's a giant planet, all right', 'Are we there yet?', 'I want an ice cream', and 'I need to go to the toilet'. The engineers can call back and say, 'You should have gone six years ago, before we left the house'.

Unless the answering machine's on the blink.

School Reports

The other day while I was ferreting around for my birth certificate to prove my existence, a hoard of old school reports tumbled from an old shoe box. I had forgotten everything, especially that in Year 7 I was the proud recipient of a 'Certificate of Commendation for Consistent Effort in French and with Percussion'.

I note that my poxy Year 7 certificate did not in any way attempt to perpetuate the filthy lie that I was any good at French or percussion (both very important life skills), just that I made some sort of tragic effort. Sadly, by Year 10 I got F for French, which was considered unsatisfactory despite the obvious fact that the word French does start with an F.

Shockingly, I deduce from one ancient document that in my last year of school I apparently promised to 'work for the well being of the school community . . . a place where Christ's life of integrity, compassion, dedication and joy is a way to be followed, not just as a distant event to be admired'. Turn it up. I also found the words to the school hymn – something to do with being cleansed of shame and sin. We weren't even Catholic, for God's sake.

In Year 8 my geography teacher wrote that I was 'ebullient and somewhat noisy' and noted that I lacked 'self-control'. Delving deeper, I found that in Year 9 I had exhibited no self-control in history, geography or 'study of society'. Were my parents supposed to infer that I had Tourette's syndrome? Was I incontinent? (I shudder to even reveal to you the utter contempt of my home economics teacher who also put a firm cross after 'courteous in speech and manner' and will explore this tragic theme in a future column.)

The report's summing-up comments try to explain: 'She must endeavour to control her talking and adopt a more mature approach'; 'It is hoped she will strive to adopt a mature approach to classroom behaviour'. The head teacher commented that this 'blemish' on my character 'should be eradicated'. It is a matter of some pride to me that I have yet to develop a mature approach. There is something about reading these judgements that fifteen years later still makes me want to run around the oval in the nuddy shouting, 'Nyah, nyah, nyahhh', shooting burning arrows into the staffroom.

In Year 10 the maths teacher thought my 'personality sometimes is the greatest obstacle for success'. (Mmm. Should I choose to be successful or have a personality?) By Year 11 my art theory teacher called me a 'conscientious wanker', but perhaps it's just bad handwriting. The French teacher questioned the wisdom of leaving the exam more than un heur before it was finis, and my politics teacher kindly claimed I had 'an independent approach to political issues'. Actually, this meant, 'she's the only raving communist greenie femmo Devil's Advocate in the class and will sometimes just completely go off like a Catherine wheel'.

How come we never got to write reports on our teachers? 'Mrs Bonce must learn to curb her talking in class'; 'Miss Volley is a huge weirdo'; 'Mr Benjamin is a great teacher and I had a major crush on him but he has proved an enormous disappointment to us all by running off to join the Liberal Party.'

Some old crinkly papers at the bottom of the shoe box reassured me that in Grade 1 I had reached a satisfactory level of personal cleanliness and had used rods in maths. The teacher did not see fit to record the incident in which she picked me up by the pigtails and deposited me IN THE RUBBISH BIN AT THE FRONT OF THE CLASS because I was caught opening a passed note saying 'Bum' on it. I will never forgive you, Miss Abyss. You suck big time. There. A student's final revenge. I feel so much more mature.

Names and Addresses

We are not a republic yet, if I may use the royal we. Until that ineluctable day, we have traditions to uphold and one of them is the maintenance of a splendid tradition, specifically and viz, the Class and Titles system of England (all stand).

Due to most regrettable recent criticism of the Governor-General giving an Australian honours medal to the Foreign Minister of Indonesia, many of you have completely forgotten your manners. As etiquette adviser to the shire council, the state government and Queen (we just call her 'Queen'), we have been asked to circulate the following list of traditional and contemporary forms of address.

(We have been assisted in this by L.G. Pine's *Guide to Titles* [1959], which states clearly, 'In ceremonial documents the Archbishop is addressed as The Most Rev. Father In God, Geoffrey, by Divine Providence Lord Archbishop of Canterbury, Primate of All England'. So if you are writing a ceremonial document for Christ's sake don't call him Geoff.)

Duke: Your Grace.
Marchioness: Your Ladyship.
Widow of a Peer: The Dowager Thing.
Archdeacon: Venerable Sir.
Governors-General: Your Excellency.
The Right Honourable, the Lord Chief Justice of England: Lordy.
The Elder Brethren of Trinity House: Captains.
The Knight of Glin: Des.

Bishop: Your Lordship.
Duke of Earl: Duke, Duke, Duke of Earl.
Knight Bachelor of the Garter: Hello, sailor.
Order of the Bath: Bubbles.
Order of the Thistle: Your Rashness.
Pope: Your Holiness.
Cardinal: Your Eminence.
Graham Richardson: Your Eminence Gris.
Australian Foreign Minister: Your Eminence Greasing.
Female Priest: Not on Your Nellyness.

Her Britannic Majesty's Envoy Extraordinary and Minister Plenipotentiary: Oh, you.
Right Worshipful, the Lord Mayor: Your Worship.
Squadron Officer: Ma'am.
Her Gracious Majesty (Queen): Your Majesty.
The Prance of Wails: Your Royal Highness.
Ordinary Citizen: Your Lowness, as unto a crawly worm.

The Prince Philip, Lieutenant Philip Mountbatten, Knight of the Garter and Duke of Edinburgh, Earl of Merioneth and Baron Greenwich: Your Royal Highness.
Servant: Your Insignificance.

Girlfriend: From a great height truly and on into Infinity, Your Magnificence and Unquenchable Fabulousness.
Boyfriend: Verily Your Adorableness and Heaven Upon a Stickiness.
Electrician: Your Incandescence.
Emperor: Your Nakedness.
A Hairy Man: Your Furness.
Crimefighter: Your Elliottness.
Environmental Activist: Your Wilderness.
Publican: Your Shout.

Game Show Host: Your Vapidness.
Dame Commander of the Royal Victorian Order: Beryl.
Retired Bishop: Right Rev. Sir.
Recently Retired Boyfriend of Woman: Right Bastard, yessir.
Retired Boyfriend of Man: His Ex-nancy.
Viscount: Sir.

In this troubling transition period, while we no longer have to pledge allegiance to Queen on Monday mornings, several other points of etiquette still apply. All letters to Peers of the Realm should be signed 'Your obedient servant'. (After the birth of the republic, this will be slightly altered to 'Later, Babe'.) At the present time, it is not permissible to touch Queen or Prince Philip (Their Royal Highnesses). After the republic, touching will be permitted. Go easy.

According to *Australian Etiquette* by Lillian Pyke (and the age of this book might be guessed at by the fact that Ms Pyke was also the author of a book called *Camp Kiddies*) it is not considered etiquette to leave calling cards at Government House, unless it is the occasion of a levee. I don't know what a levee is, but I believe you are supposed to take a Chevy to it, and by all accounts, probably a bottle.

'On special occasions in the country,' suggests Lillian, 'the Governor-General and his wife are sometimes entertained.' (On most occasions feel free to bore them rigid.) There is seldom any excuse for not accepting invitations to Government House. Women should curtsey to the Governor-General and his wife. (A curtsey is performed by firmly grasping the hem of your frock, bobbing down slightly, balancing on your back foot, throwing the skirt above your head and shouting, 'All Hail the Excellencies!'. Inevitably this will sound rather muffled, but no less heartfelt.)

Further instructions will be issued in the event of a republic.